CONSERVATIVES ARE FROM

MARS,

LIBERALS ARE FROM

San Francisco

CONSERVATIVES ARE FROM

MARS,

LIBERALS ARE FROM

San Francisco

101 REASONS WHY I'M HAPPY
I LEFT THE LEFT

Burt Prelutsky

CUMBERLAND HOUSE
NASHVILLE, TENNESSEE

CONSERVATIVES ARE FROM MARS, LIBERALS ARE FROM SAN FRANCISCO
Published by Cumberland House Publishing, Inc.
431 Harding Industrial Drive
Nashville, TN 37211-3160

Cover design: James Duncan
Text design: Julie Pitkin

Library of Congress Cataloging-in-Publication Data
Prelutsky, Burt, 1940–
    Conservatives are from Mars, liberals are from San Francisco : 101 reasons why
I'm happy I left the left / Burt Prelutsky ; foreword by Bernard Goldberg.
        p. cm.
    ISBN-13: 978-1-58182-571-8 (pbk. : alk. paper)
    ISBN-10: 1-58182-571-4 (pbk. : alk. paper)
    1. American wit and humor. 2. Liberalism—United States—Humor. I. Title.

    PN6165.P74 2006
    814'.54—dc22

                                                                          2006024652

Printed in the United States of America
1 2 3 4 5 6 7—12 11 10 09 08 07 06

Thanks to Yvonne, who manages the impossible—
to share both my politics and my life. Simply amazing.

Thanks to all my friends and loved ones for being my friends and
loved ones, sometimes in spite of our politics.

And thanks to America's liberals just for being themselves—
and thus providing me with all my very best lines.

Contents

Foreword

I've never spent much time thinking about reincarnation. Don't get me wrong; if you want to believe that you're coming back as a chicken or a turtle or Barbra Streisand after you die, be my guest. Live and let live is my motto. Even when you're dead.

But now I'm having second thoughts. Now, I think I'm turning into a believer. Because now I have reason to suspect that Mark Twain may have come back. Not as one of his leaping frogs of Calaveras County or anything like that, but that he somehow pulled a few strings with whomever's in charge of such things and managed to return as an updated version of his old self, as a witty and perceptive chronicler of the great American scene.

But for show business reasons he changed his name. Now he goes by Burt Prelutsky.

I got to know Burt slowly, over many years, one witty and perceptive essay at a time. His writing made so much sense. And like a great center fielder, he made it all look easy. That, probably more than anything else, is why I detest him. It's why I loathe him to this day. No one should be this good, this often, and make it look like he isn't even breaking a sweat.

Nevertheless, despite my contempt for the author (which only *looks* like envy), this collection of essays on everything from neighbors and old movies to Hitler — passing references to the Three Musketeers, Rocky Balboa, Superman, and Hillary Clinton — is a triumph of common sense over the foolishness we see all around us in America these days. Burt sticks pins in all the right bubbles. In one piece about attorneys, he asks a good question: "How is it that in a society in which everything from toys to toasters comes with dire warnings attached, lawyers don't?"

In an essay about Islamic terrorists, he writes, "What I find most disconcerting about these Muslims is that they almost manage to make Nazis look normal by comparison."

On the differences between the genders, Burt observes: "Men think women are loco. Women think the same about men. News flash: They're both right. They just happen to be loony in different ways. Men, for instance, actually think it's important who coaches the Notre Dame football team. Women, on the other hand, will write mash notes to convicted killers."

In the title piece of this collection, "Conservatives Are From Mars, Liberals Are From San Francisco" — not just a great title, but a better one, in my opinion, than *Hamlet,* which I always found a bit flat — Burt captures the whole sorry, snobby, hypocritical mess that has become modern day liberalism. "And isn't it strange," he writes, "that although it's those on the left who constantly claim they're the ones looking out for the poor, the oppressed, the disenfranchised, I've often heard liberals dismiss 250 million of their fellow Americans as 'those people we fly over' when going from L.A. to New York, I swear I've never heard a similar remark from a conservative."

On race, he points out, "Liberals always boast that theirs is a party of inclusion, proudly boasting that they're home for the likes of Maxine Waters, Al Sharpton, and Jesse Jackson — three people most of us wouldn't even want to have over for dinner..." But bring up the name of Clarence Thomas or Condoleezza Rice or radio talk show host Larry Elder or any black person, for that matter, who "doesn't toe the party line, and the hounds of the left can be counted on to start barking, 'Oreo,' 'Uncle Tom,' and 'Sell Out.'"

This is how Burt sums up the "tolerant" left on the subject of religion: "Liberals, often under the banner of the ACLU, will lead the charge for religious freedom. But when you check the record, you find that the religious practices they defend tend to be those that involve the smoking of marijuana, the ingesting of peyote buttons, and the ritualistic slaughtering of small animals. Where they draw the line is when it comes to the barbaric practices of hanging Christmas wreaths and lighting menorahs."

Referring to left-of-center cultural elitists, Tom Wolfe, the great author and journalist, spoke for many of us when he said, "There is something in me that particularly wants it registered that I am not one of them."

Rest assured, Burt Prelutsky is not one of them either. As he sums up at the end of his title essay: "Most of the conservatives I know, including myself, started out somewhere else on the political spectrum, and evolved through time and knowledge and experience. I personally do not know of a single case of an individual evolving in the other direction. I will leave it to the Darwinists to make of that what they will."

The other Mark Twain couldn't have said it better.

— *Bernard Goldberg*

Acknowledgments

I wish to acknowledge those stalwart souls without whose contributions this book would probably not exist. In alphabetical order, they are Andrew Alexander, Jim Bass, Gregory Borse, Christopher Cook, Reginald Firehammer, Jonathan Garthwaite, Mike LaSalle, Ron Strom, and Nicholas Winter.

And finally, I wish to express my thanks to those folks without whose efforts this book would definitely not exist. Their names are Ken Fong, Joseph Farah, Craig Wiley, and Ron Pitkin.

CONSERVATIVES ARE FROM

MARS,

LIBERALS ARE FROM

San Francisco

Chapter One

HOLLYWOOD: THE LAND WHERE PYGMIES THINK THEY'RE GIANTS BECAUSE THEY LOOK SO DARN BIG ON THE MOVIE SCREEN

• 1 •
Reviewing Movies I Haven't Seen

It's been 48 years since I last reviewed a movie without first seeing it. Back then, a fellow UCLA student, Shirley Mae Follmer, and I were competing to be the film critic for the *Daily Bruin*. One night, passes were supposed to be left for each of us at a press screening. However, she arrived ahead of me, and she had either brought a guest along or there had simply been a glitch somewhere along the line. In any case, they wouldn't let me in. All I knew was the title of the movie and the name of the star, but I wasn't about to go down without a fight. So I went home and wrote an amusing review of a musical trifle with Mario Lanza called *The Seven Hills of Rome*.

Needless to say, I got the gig. To be fair, Shirley was at a disadvantage. By the time she had sat through the movie and gone home, it was probably eleven o'clock. I had already written my review and gone beddy-bye by then.

I spent the next 13 years atoning for my minor sin by reviewing movies for the *Bruin* and for *Los Angeles* magazine. Inasmuch as those years included the entire decade of the '60s, a terrible time for movies, I would say that, for once, the punishment far exceeded the crime.

I'm afraid that it is time for me to once again review, not just one, but two movies I have no intention of seeing. I am only doing it because people keep asking me what I think of *Munich* and *Brokeback Mountain*. I have finally decided that not seeing them shouldn't prevent my having an opinion. So, for the record, I don't like them.

No doubt some of you are shaking your heads in annoyance. Where the heck do I get off panning two major motion pictures when I've only seen their coming attractions? Well, for one thing, I have read so much about them, pro and con, that I feel as if I've seen them. For another, I have learned to trust my instincts. I have never liked a Steven Spielberg movie, and I have seen most of *them*. I'm willing to accept that he's as gifted a moviemaker as his fans and flacks say, but I just didn't care for *Jaws, Close Encounters of the Third Kind, E.T., The Color Purple, Saving Private Ryan,* or even *Schindler's List.*

As if that wasn't bad enough, he hired two guys named Tony Kushner and Eric Roth to write the script. Kushner made his big splash with *Angels in America,* and Roth won his Oscar for *Forrest Gump.* The truth is, I saw both and could barely keep my eyes open during either of them.

So when I read that in Kushner's never-humble opinion, Israel is an unfortunate blemish on the face of the earth, and I know that Spielberg has said that the seven or eight hours he spent chatting with Fidel Castro were the most important hours of his life, I had a pretty good hunch that I would not enjoy their collaborative effort. When I then read time and again that Spielberg regards Israel's execution of Palestinian terrorists to be the moral equivalent of the butchery those Muslims committed at the Munich Olympics, I see no compelling reason to ignore my instincts and race down to the local Bijou.

This brings us to *Brokeback Mountain.* I happen to be one of those wimps who really has a live-and-let-live attitude where gays are concerned. What they do to and with one another is none of my business just so long as I don't have to watch it. But from what I hear, this movie leaves very little to the imagination. And, frankly, when I go to a movie, I'd really rather not be reminded that I have an appointment coming up soon with my proctologist.

I have friends who have avoided the movie because they fear it might forever ruin cowboy movies for them. As I've never been a big fan of the genre, having only liked a handful of westerns in my entire life, I didn't share that particular concern. Instead, I have given *Brokeback* a wide berth because I suspect most of the raves for it are coming from people who want to prove how sophisticated and broad-minded they are. I just can't help thinking that what Katherine Hepburn said about *Midnight Cowboy,* another over-hyped movie that neither of us liked, she might well have said about *Brokeback Mountain:* "If the movie had been about a boy and a girl, instead of two boys, everybody would have realized it was a stinker!"

• 2 •

In Defense of Hollywood

There are a lot of people whose favorite sport is taking pot shots at the film industry. They enjoy pointing out that the actresses are as vain as peacocks, spending more on botox, collagen, and plastic surgery in a month than most normal people spend on food, rent, and clothes in a decade.

They like to point out that actors, whose formal education often ended with high school and whose reading is pretty much limited to movie scripts and *Daily Variety,* mouth off about politics and sundry matters as if they were the intellectual equals of Charles Krauthammer and Thomas Sowell.

But I am here not to bury Hollywood, as it were, but to praise it.

For instance, one criticism you often hear leveled at the industry is that it is solely money-driven and that artistic considerations take a back seat to the bottom line. That simply is not the case. If it were, do you think for a moment that Hollywood would have produced so many movies about drug addicts over the years, or that directors like Otto Preminger and Robert Altman would have enjoyed such long, unprofitable careers?

Or, consider, if you will, movies with gay characters. With the exception of *The Bird Cage,* a mediocre remake of the French *La Cage aux Folles,* the American public has shown little interest in being exposed to a lifestyle which, in the main, it barely tolerates but hardly endorses. And yet, gay-themed movies continue to be churned out.

I realize that some folks will suggest that *Brokeback Mountain* was a hit. It certainly made a big noise in the media, but not at the box office. Even with all the attention focused on it, in a time when even a moderately successful movie breaks the inflation-inflated domestic gross mark of $100 million, *Brokeback* won't even come close.

Some people insist that Hollywood is filled with arrogant jerks who make Narcissus look modest by comparison. But down deep, even the biggest stars are eager to be friendly and are very, very human. For instance, for the opportunity to have lunch with Steven Spielberg, date Pamela Anderson, or sit courtside, next to Jack Nicholson, at a Laker game, most of them would drive their SUVs over their own grandmothers.

The idea that Hollywood only cares about profits is totally off the mark. Various political and social agendas are of far greater importance in the general scheme of things. If it comes down to producing a hit or promoting a cause — be it pro-socialism, anti-capitalism, pro-Arab, or anti-Israel — it is invariably a case of damn the accountants, full speed ahead! The truth is, one could almost make a case for Hollywood's being opposed to the profit system. Consider animated movies, if you will. For decades, from the time that Walt Disney invented the art form, the actors who gave voice to the likes of Cinderella, Bambi, Dumbo, Pinocchio, and Snow White were as anonymous as the men and women who painted the cels. They did their jobs just fine, and, moreover, they worked cheap. Which, of course, meant more money for Uncle Walt. Best of all, unlike the other studio moguls, he didn't have to deal with his stars' agents or their egos; when the movie was over, all he had to do was erase the entire cast. But somewhere along the line, some yutz decided they needed big names supplying the voices of those cartoon characters. One can only assume that the guy was as star-struck as some hayseed on a tour bus and simply hankered for the opportunity to rub elbows with the likes of Tom Hanks, Billy Crystal, Whoopi Goldberg, and Robin Williams. For whatever reason, the budgets for these cartoon movies suddenly jumped $20 million or so. Does that sound to you like a cold-blooded business run by a bunch of penny-pinching bean-counters? I think we can all agree that Hollywood wears its heart on its sleeve, even if it keeps its brain in the cookie jar. Only a bunch of old softies could convince themselves that there's anybody in the entire world who actually cares whose voice they're listening to when they go to see *Shrek* or *Toy Story.* That's what I believe, and I'll continue to believe it until somebody swears to me that their spouse actually ran into the house and yelled, "Grab the kids, sweetheart! We're all going to the cineplex to *hear* Ray Romano's new movie!"

• 3 •

The Horror!

I had thought the Left had finally run out of preposterous things to say about President Bush. I mean, between Dan Rather, Chris Matthews, Charlie Sheen, Howard Dean, John Kerry, Al Gore, Helen Thomas, and the rest of the card-carrying liberal loonies, what was left to be said about the man? That he slurped his soup? That he hated John Wayne westerns? That he beat up Laura on a regular basis?

These people who would rush to defend Osama bin Laden, arguing that he must have been potty-trained too early, and defend Satan on the grounds that anyone would be justified in acting up if they'd been booted out of Heaven, can't even bring themselves to say something nice about the way Bush dresses.

The latest attack on the president was so bizarre that when I first heard it, my immediate reaction was to laugh. It certainly sounded like a piece of dialogue that a conservative writer might stick in the mouth of a liberal character in a political satire. But I quickly realized that 34-year-old writer-director Eli Roth was serious when he told Neal Cavuto that George W. Bush was responsible for the rash of horror movies turned out by Hollywood in recent years.

It's easy enough to dismiss the ravings of the over-wrought Mr. Roth when he contends that when there's horror in the world, which there is thanks to Bush's policies, people feel the need to scream. And the one socially acceptable place to do it, Roth explained to Cavuto, is at the local cineplex.

Roth, whose few credits include *Cabin Fever* and *Hostel,* a couple of low-budget horror flicks that will make nobody forget *Casablanca* or *Citizen Kane,* managed in just a few ill-chosen words to display his arrogance and his ignorance.

He went on in a feeble attempt to give his inane comments historical perspective by insisting there was also a spate of horror movies during the Vietnam War. Well, it's true that between, say, '63 and '73, there were a bunch of them. But there were also a slew between '23 and '33, '33 and '43, and so on. What's more, it didn't make a smidgen of difference if a Democrat or a Republican was living in the White House.

Perhaps Mr. Roth, who wasn't born until '72, is unaware of a major movie star named Lon Chaney. Even President Bush wasn't alive when Chaney was terrifying the movie-going public in such silent films as *The Unholy Three, The Unknown,* and *Phantom of the Opera,* all made during a time of peace and prosperity.

Some sense of the way audiences of every era have clamored after movie chills can be derived from the fact that *Phantom* was remade on seven separate occasions between 1943 and 1999 — not counting Andrew Lloyd Webber's musical.

Once the sound era rolled around, you couldn't stop the deluge. And it didn't matter if the country was at peace or at war, no matter the state of the economy. Just a few of them were *Jekyll and Hyde, Dracula, Frankenstein, Freaks, The Wolfman, Cat People, The Picture of Dorian Gray, The Creature From the Black Lagoon, The Blob, The Thing, Phantom of the Rue Morgue, Night of the Living Dead,* and *Psycho.* But it was in the '70s and '80s that the stream of dreck reached flood level with the likes of *Night Terrors, The Omen, The Other, Eaten Alive, The Texas Chain Saw Massacre, Scream, Halloween,* and *A Nightmare on Elm Street.* And like the creatures that often populated these turkeys, many of these movies birthed monstrous offspring, better known as sequels. The worst thing, though, about Mr. Roth's puerile attack on the president is his obvious lack of gratitude. I mean, if he actually believes Bush is personally responsible for there being an audience for his infantile claptrap, you'd think he'd have the decency to send the man candy and flowers instead of brickbats. As I see it, the real problem with most of the product Hollywood churns out these days isn't that they're horror flicks, but that they're just plain horrible. And for that, President Bush is entirely blameless. And if Mr. Roth really wants to find a villain, he need only stop gazing through his viewfinder and look in the mirror.

• 4 •

Hollywood:
Land of the Useless Idiots

When I titled my book *Conservatives Are From Mars, Liberals Are From San Francisco,* I could just as easily have pointed out that liberals are from Hollywood. It really is a different planet from the one most of us live on.

To begin with, it is populated with high school dropouts and drama majors making millions of dollars a year, convinced they should decide how the rest of us think, live, and vote. What you must never forget about these pampered pets is that the first lesson they learned in acting class was to get in touch with their feelings. Those self-absorbing exercises only served to diminish whatever thought processes they might have possessed. The end result is that, at their best, they can mimic emotions and action but have an impossible time trying to suggest they are thinking about anything at all, except for the size of their trailers and their back-end points.

Never forget that the things we see on the screen are shadows. The real articles are people who spend their lives wearing other people's clothes, mouthing other people's lines, and being told how to walk and talk by directors. They should come with warning labels stating that, for all their fame and fortune, they are as bright as department store mannequins.

This past election was the most bitterly fought in memory, but nowhere was it waged more vituperatively than in Hollywood. In recent months, lifelong friendships have been torn asunder. Just this morning, I heard about a poker game involving writers and producers that had weathered 20 years of trials and tribulations but could not survive George W. Bush's re-election.

One thing you have to give Hollywood celebrities credit for is their monumental gall. I mean, Barbra Streisand insults conservatives more often than she bathes, knowing full well it won't harm her CD sales. Julia Roberts announces that if you look up Republican in the dictionary, you'll find it right after reptiles, and yet she continues selling movie tickets, even though 52% of the electorate cast their ballots for George Bush.

You'll notice that show biz liberals are very outspoken, just so long as they're addressing the choir. But you rarely see them placing themselves in a situation where they have to debate the issues. Have you ever once seen Michael Moore addressing any groups that didn't consist of either American college students or French film snobs? No, neither have I. Some years ago, long before Alzheimers set in, Charlton Heston offered to debate Ms. Streisand on the subject of gun ownership, all the money collected to go to the charity of her choice. Naturally, the debate never took place.

If you do not live in L.A., you can not imagine the grief that descended upon this community on November 3rd. How could Hollywood's glitterati not take John Kerry's defeat personally? After all, for the past year, people like Billy Crystal, Whoopi Goldberg, Alec Baldwin, Tim Robbins, Susan Sarandon, and the rest of the usual suspects, had taken time out of their busy, privileged lives to help elect Kerry. Like children anticipating a white Christmas, they were imagining themselves speed-dialing the White House for the next four, maybe eight, years, inviting John and Teresa to movie premieres and weekends at the Springs. How dare those "folks we fly over" spoil their plans?

These people live in such a cocoon that they, quite literally, do not have dealings with people who are not in lockstep with them. A few years ago, a friend of mine and his wife were invited to a cocktail party. Several other guests had already arrived before they got there. As they entered a fairly crowded den, a very successful TV producer was telling the group that he, personally, did not know a single a**hole who had voted for Bush. My friend, with perfect timing, said, "Well, you do now."

Alfre Woodard's contention that her colleagues in SAG are "informed, compassionate and articulate," aside, the sheep of Hollywood are more likely to question the deaths of James Dean, Marilyn Monroe, and Elvis Presley than they are to seriously question a single plank of the Democratic platform. And, being the self-righteous boors they are, they never see any contradiction between the populist pap they parrot and the way they actually live their lives.

For my part, the election results provided me with a euphoria the Hollywood crowd only gets to experience when one of their movies cracks the $100 million barrier at the box office or when someone else's movie doesn't. And when the high threatens to wear off, I merely have to think of yet another Hollywood gasbag who must really be in the dumps these days. Just recently, I thought about Bill Maher and felt terrific for the rest of the day.

Before the election of 2004, as with every election for at least the past 40 years, we all had to listen to the liberals vow that if the Republican won, they were moving en masse to New Zealand. Well, I'm taking this occasion to announce that I stand ready to shuttle them, one and all, to LAX for the next one-way flight to Wellington.

• 5 •
Football, Baseball, and the Movies

Whenever I speak to a group of writers, I can bank on someone's asking where I get my ideas. My usual glib reply is that I count on ideas finding me because I'm just too darn lazy to go searching for them. In a way, that happens to be the truth. More often than not, I'll be driving down the street and some odd thought will pop into my head. Then the trick is to remember it long enough to jot myself a note.

After a while, I've got a bunch of these little pieces of paper collected, all of them filled with scribbled, somewhat cryptic, messages to myself. As a rule, if I don't turn them into an essay within a week or so, I find I never will. On the other hand, I hate just tossing them away. Instead, periodically, I salvage some for a smorgasbord. So, here are a few Swedish meatballs for you to nibble on.

Somebody, I've decided, should do something about the scoring system in football. I'm already on record as being opposed to touchdowns counting for six — actually seven — points. It misleads people into thinking that football has more offense than baseball, when in fact a 28-14 game means there were only six scores, not 42.

And speaking of extra points, isn't it high time they got rid of them? The kick is nearly automatic, and all it does is waste everyone's time. Let them run it in or pass it in for a point, if they must, as they presently do for two points.

Furthermore, it makes no sense that a 20-yard field goal counts the same as a 50 or 60-yarder. For that matter, I'd award bonus points for an 85-yard punt return or a 92-yard run for a touchdown.

And why should a one-yard plunge by a 260-pound fullback count for as much as a 70-yard reception? I might even award points to the defense for goal line stands.

While on the subject of sports, I'll try to explain why I am the only person I know who likes George Steinbrenner. Mainly, I appreciate the fact that he takes his role as keeper of the flame as seriously as he does. In everything he does, from maintaining Monument Park in center field as a memorial to former Yankee greats, to staging the classiest old-timers games in baseball, to hiring the very best broadcasting crew, he expresses his respect for the game. Those who whine about the money he spends on players seem to overlook the fact that it's his dough. Also, unlike all the other money-grubbing owners in professional sports, when Steinbrenner decided to build a new stadium, he didn't blackmail the taxpayers into footing the bill. As usual, he's paying for it out of his own pocket.

Another thing I like about the man is that no matter how much he's willing to pay for talent, he refuses to negotiate when it comes to facial hair. He forked over $135 million for Jason Giambi, but the goatee had to go. Frankly, I don't understand all the silly-looking beards that have sprouted in the major leagues over the past decade. I really don't know what it is with these guys, but they must be the only people in America who think the Amish are a bunch of hotties.

Finally, it occurs to me that while most Americans are aware that in their values and their politics, Hollywood's liberals are quite different from themselves, they don't know the half of it.

For instance, most people are unaware that although movies are a business, there's probably no other commercial enterprise that's run on such an un-businesslike basis.

Consider, if you will, that the majority of movies lose money. What's more, an average twelve-year-old could probably predict which of them will definitely fail. So the question is, why produce them? Well, part of the reason is that far too many of the people who develop movie projects aren't developing them for the general public, but for each other. When they get together for lunch or cocktails, they don't want to appear square. It would kill them to say they're green-lighting a family flick, even though year in and year out it's G-rated movies that dominate the market.

Instead, these black-clad young executives, men and women alike, prefer to boast that they've got something dark and edgy in the works, something, they love to say, that really pushes the envelope.

As a result, at any given time, you can count on there being half a dozen movies dealing with dope addicts in production, even though *The Man With the Golden Arm,* made back in 1955, was probably the last druggie movie to make a dollar — and that one starred Frank Sinatra and Kim Novak, not Gary Oldman and Willem Dafoe, for crying out loud.

So, why, if they consistently lose money, do they keep producing these grungy movies about heroin addicts, hookers, and other assorted lowlifes? For the same reason that normal people make home movies. They just like to see themselves on screen.

Chapter Two

SURE, GIVE US YOUR POOR, YOUR HUDDLED MASSES, BUT MUST THEY ALL BE MEXICANS?

• 6 •
My Good Neighbor Policy

As every real estate agent will tell you, the value of any property inevitably comes down to three things. Namely, location, location, location.

Usually, they're talking about accessibility to shops, schools, and the work place. Sometimes, of course, it means the house has a nice view or it sits on a large corner lot or, at the very least, isn't situated too close to an airport or a toxic dump.

The one thing that rarely gets mentioned is, in the long run, the most important thing of all. I refer to the neighbors. After all, it's not that big a deal if you have to drive another couple of blocks to the supermarket or the local cineplex. But anybody who has ever wound up living next door to an obnoxious neighbor will tell you it casts a pall on one's very existence, no matter how many bathrooms you have and no matter how spectacular the view.

Whether the problem is his barking dog or the drunken parties or merely his cranky personality, you will soon find yourself lying awake night after night plotting how to murder the guy in ways so wily that even Sherlock Holmes would be stumped as to the means, if not the motive.

What has me thinking along these lines isn't my own neighbors, fortunately, but America's. My neighbors, I'm happy to report, are swell people. They're friendly, decent folks I'm sure I could count on in a pinch. America, on the other hand, is stuck with Canada and Mexico. They're the sort who let their dogs do their business on your front lawn and who play bad music so loudly that it makes your entire house vibrate and your poor ears beg for mercy.

Canada, I must confess, is the bigger surprise of the two. We all know that our huge but under-populated neighbor to the north suffers from an inferiority complex as big as the Yukon. It's understandable. Year after year, it sees its best and its brightest moving south. Those who stay put know in their hearts that they have settled for being big fish in a small pond. Worst of all, even their hockey teams are no longer better than ours.

Still, who would have guessed that their resentment was so deep-rooted that when it came to the recent unpleasantness with Saddam Hussein, they would side with the sorry likes of Germany, France, Russia and China, against not only the U.S., but their British and Australian cousins?

Which brings us, alas, to Mexico, a country that has benefited not only from favorable trade agreements with us, but from the largesse of the Yankee taxpayer for a depressingly long time.

Our politicians have long pandered for Chicano votes by forgiving billion-dollar debts, turning a blind eye to illegal aliens and drug trafficking, granting amnesty with a disgusting regularity, and by treating President Fox with the sort of consideration usually reserved for rich relatives.

In return, Mexico not only voted against us as a member of the U.N. Security Council, but has granted sanctuary to well over a hundred fugitives on the lam from American justice. Mexico, a country well known for its corrupt cops and its vicious penal system, oddly enough refuses to extradite anyone facing the possibility of execution. As a result, it has become a haven for murderers and sexual predators fleeing their just desserts. One can't help but wonder why our judges continue to grant bail in such cases. And in those instances where we haven't yet captured the good-for-nothing, why don't we tell the Mexican authorities that they're only wanted for traffic violations?

All that being the case, what can we to do to improve our living arrangements? Well, when very rich people find themselves living next door to those they dislike or are merely seeking a bit more privacy, what they often do, at least here in Southern California, is buy their neighbor's house. Then, to ensure that they never have the problem in the future, they simply tear down the dwelling and plant flowers.

Well, America is certainly rich enough. So the only questions, so far as I can see, are what do you think it would cost to buy Canada and Mexico, and do you prefer roses or petunias?

• 7 •

Dear Congressman

If nobody has ever suggested that when you have a politician for a friend, you don't need any enemies, let me be the first.

The politician I have in mind has been a chum ever since college days. Although he has held elected office for the past thirty-four years, I have always told people that Mickey (not his real name) was the most unassuming guy you'd ever want to meet. If you didn't know he was a U.S. congressman, the chances are he'd never get around to telling you.

Anyway, a few weeks ago, I discovered that our neighbors here in the San Fernando Valley had put their home up for sale. When I asked them why, they explained that they had been lying to their daughter's school, Coolidge High, about where they lived. Some of the girl's friends had already been expelled when their parents had been unable to prove that they actually lived in the Encino school district. Rather than wait for the ax to drop, they were looking to move.

The reality, however, was that because of the differential in real estate values, even if my neighbors got their asking price, they didn't see how they could afford to buy in Encino. It was Catch-22 for civilians.

If they did nothing, their daughter would have to transfer to Cabrillo High, which is ninety percent Hispanic and is far inferior, academically speaking.

The only thing I could think to do was write to my favorite congressman. I was pretty certain it was a waste of time, but I figured there was always an outside chance that Mickey would know some-body who knew somebody who could make a phone call. So I dropped him a line, spelling out the problem that these "poor, decent, hard-working people" were having because they were trying to provide a better education for their daughter.

He promptly wrote back to say that I was right, that there wasn't anything he could do. But then he went on: "When you have time, Burt, maybe you can explain the difference between your poor, decent, hard-working family that only wants a better education for their daughter, but has lied about where they actually live; and the poor, decent, hard-working family that sneaks across the border because they want a better education for their daughter."

Frankly, my friends, I was astonished. More than that, I was shocked and appalled. It was just such an unlikely response from my old pal, a fellow who, in spite of our political differences, has always struck me as being smart, sensible, and amusing. When I realized that on this occasion he wasn't being any of those three things, and had actually taken the opportunity to climb aboard his moral high horse, I felt I had no option but to set him straight.

"Dear Mickey," I wrote, "I am always ready to answer any of your questions. This happens to be a particularly easy one. For one thing, 'my family' are American citizens. Their taxes not only go to support both high schools, but help pay your salary.

"Next, their offense consisted of lying about where they lived because they saw no compelling reason why their child should suf-fer scholastically just because they happened to live a few blocks northeast of some arbitrarily-drawn boundary. 'Your family,' on the other hand, were sneaks whose first act upon entering this country was to break a federal law. How on earth do you find these two acts morally or legally comparable?

"Furthermore, as 'my family' is relatively poor, they are unable to send their child to a private school as you, a leading proponent of public education, have sent all three of yours. And as you are joined at the hip with the likes of Boxer, Feinstein, and Pelosi, you are naturally opposed to vouchers — vouchers which would have enabled these people to send the girl to a nearby, but pricey, religious school."

In conclusion, I wrote: "The most shameful aspect of all this is my realization that Coolidge High clearly protects its sovereignty with far greater diligence than you and your colleagues protect America's."

It's been over a month now. Mickey hasn't gotten back to me.

• 8 •

In Defense of Fences

Recently, I attended a conference headed up by the great Ward Connerly. Over the two days, a great many issues were discussed by the group. The participants weren't exactly a cross-section of the general public, consisting, as the gathering did, of lawyers, academics, successful businessmen, and me.

Although there were divided opinions on all the issues, the one that created the most heat and, I suspect, the least light was the matter of illegal immigrants. You couldn't even get everybody to agree it was a problem. For those who favored open borders, "undocumented workers" was the term of choice. In the end, it all came down to the same old liberal/conservative argument.

Those whose attitude can best be summed up as "the more the merrier" accuse the opposition of being racist. Those on the other side argue that a nation without borders is no nation at all, but merely a state of mind.

Just last week, I was arguing the issue with a friend. I pointed out that every other country in the world guards its borders, and that definitely includes Mexico, which protects its own southern border while violating our own on a daily basis. He said he didn't care what other countries did. He believed that America, being America, should have a welcome mat out for anyone who wants to enter. He didn't want to slam the door in the face of poor people.

I told him he was a hypocrite. After all, I knew for a fact that he had locks on the windows and doors of his home. Why shouldn't poor people be allowed to enter his dwelling and set up housekeeping in his living room? By what right should he have greater authority over his property than the nation has over its own?

I live in Los Angeles, haven to hundreds of thousands of illegal immigrants. It is also the place that Cardinal Mahony, defender of pedophile priests, calls home. Any time a local politician suggests that illegals are coarsening the quality of life in our community while crowding our schools and overwhelming our health care resources, Mahony can be counted on to label the man a racist. Like an actor responding to his cue, Mahony will insist that these are all hard-working Mexicans who are only looking to share in the American dream. But does anyone really believe that Mahony or any of his colleagues in the Catholic hierarchy, all of them looking to fill church pews, would give a damn how hard-working those border sneaks were if they happened to be Lutherans?

Those who condemn us, the anti-illegal crowd, as racists are always contending we wouldn't be so anxious to defend our borders if those were Swedes coming across. The truth is, illegals are illegal, and I don't happen to care what nationality they are. I simply have a bone to pick with anybody whose first act on American soil is to break the law. There are, after all, millions of people all over the world waiting their turn to emigrate legally. When you get right down to it, it's those who constantly argue on behalf of Latinos for no other reason than their race who are the real racists.

To put this problem in some perspective, a conservative estimate of the number of illegal Hispanics in America is 10 million. But not this conservative's. I'm guessing it's at least twice that many. But even if it were 10 million, in order to match that number, not only would every single Swede have to pack up and sneak over, but they'd have to bring a few million Norwegians along with them.

Instead of honestly debating the issue, liberals prefer to quote Emma Lazarus on the subject. "Give me your tired, your poor, /Your huddled masses yearning to breathe free,/The wretched refuse of your teeming shore..." That works fine in the context of legal immigration. But the last time I looked, there was nothing in there that said, "Let those fortunate enough to share our borders sneak in ahead of everybody else. They don't have to play by the same rules as Poles and Kenyans and Koreans. So long as they speak Spanish, they get a free pass."

And let us keep in mind that what Miss Lazarus was writing was a little poem, not national policy.

• 9 •

The United States of Mexico

Sometimes, when I hear people objecting to illegal aliens on the grounds that they represent a security risk, I find myself shaking my head. To me, that sounds as if they wouldn't have a problem with America's porous southern border if only it weren't for the tragic events of 9/11. The implication is that we wouldn't object to all those millions of people sneaking into our country, except for those few bad apples who might be looking to level Los Angeles with a suitcase bomb.

These folks are entitled to their opinion, but they certainly don't speak for me. My objection is based on the fact that I don't like unwelcome guests. I don't like them in my house, and I don't want them in my country.

Because we're speaking, for the most part, about Mexicans, that opens me up to a charge of racism. So be it. In a society in which such repulsive characters as Barry Bonds, Cynthia McKinney, Jesse Jackson, Al Sharpton, Harry Belafonte, and O.J. Simpson deflect all manner of criticism by attributing it to white racists, the word has lost virtually all meaning.

I happen to like Mexicans. Living here in the San Fernando Valley, I interact with them all the time. Several of them live on my block. I find them, by and large, to be a virtuous people. They tend to be hard-working, religious, family-oriented, and friendly. Although I'm not a big fan of refried beans and rice, I do like their music. Unlike the anti-social, unaesthetic dreck that usually passes for music these days, most Mexican songs seem to be love ballads.

What's more, thanks to church influence, their young people tend to get married and to raise their kids together. I do wish, however, that, as a group, the youngsters were as enthusiastic about attending classes as they are about ditching class to take part in public demonstrations.

All of that said, I am in favor of building a wall, digging a moat, doing whatever it takes to keep illegals out.

I understand that President Bush has a problem dealing with this problem. There are businesses, after all, that depend on a constant stream of unskilled workers. I say constant because we already have several million illegal aliens in America — surely enough to pick our lettuce, bus our tables, wash our cars, and put the little mints on our hotel pillows. But this is the land of opportunity, and people don't want to remain very long at the bottom of the food chain.

So George Bush promotes a worker program that is so idiotic, Republicans wish that a Democrat had come up with it so they'd feel better about ridiculing it. Suggesting that after working in this country for a number of years, Mexicans will simply return to their country and take their place at the back of the immigration line is perhaps the single stupidest, most naïve notion I've ever heard. Even a four-year-old would recognize Bush's brainstorm as amnesty in sheep's clothing.

People who disagree with me on this issue point out that if I were a Mexican, I'd also do whatever I could to get into this country. And they're right. Walk across the desert? You bet! To get to America, I'd walk across ground glass. But, so what? What I would or wouldn't do is no basis upon which to form national policy.

It's high time that the president stopped pandering to special interests and instead started acting like a man who can afford to have principles. Otherwise, what's the point of being a lame duck? It seems to me there should be some upside to never again having to worry about being re-elected.

If Bush drew a line in the sand — and then built a wall on that line — I'm betting he'd even see his poll numbers bounce up. As a result of which, he might actually stop being a political liability as the GOP gears up for the congressional elections in November.

If Bush asked for my advice, I'd tell him it's time he stopped listening to President Fox and started listening to the American people. And then I'd point out to him that nowhere in the Constitution does it say it's his responsibility to cure Mexico's crime and unemployment problems.

• 10 •

Time to Wake Up and Smell the Salsa

I understand that George Bush and his Republican colleagues think they can have it both ways with this so-called guest worker program. Well, they can't. Gussy it up any which way you like, it's still amnesty. And like Reagan's amnesty program of '86, it will be another disaster for America.

Either the GOP is for more and more Mexicans coming across the border or it's not. But they should be warned that if it's the former, they run the very real risk of eliminating themselves as a major political party. Even though I realize that taking a strong, principled stand on this issue could alienate certain major business interests and the Catholic hierarchy, I'm convinced that not doing so will constitute political suicide.

A few years ago, I suggested that if Republican challenger Bill Simon were to have any shot at unseating California's inept governor, Gray Davis, he had to come out forcefully against the epidemic that was bleeding California's schools, health services, and prisons dry of much needed funds. Simon, a man with the looks and charisma of Mortimer Snerd, came surprisingly close, losing by a scant four percent. I have no doubt he would have won if he'd taken my advice. By not daring to risk offending the Hispanic voters, who naturally went overwhelmingly for the Democrat anyway, Simon merely gave the state's conservatives a good excuse to stay home on election day.

Any Republican who believes that turning a blind eye to the problem will generate boundless gratitude among Mexican voters is probably the same sort of pinhead who harbors the hope that blacks and Jews will soon be lining up to join the party. Being as stupid as they are, perhaps it wouldn't be such a tragedy if they disappeared from the political landscape, going the way of the dodo and other inferior species.

We keep hearing how essential the guest worker program is to our financial well-being.

If the ruling class really wanted to do something substantive along those lines, there are a couple of things that come to mind. First off, they should deport the directors of every company that moves its factories overseas. Let these greedy pigs go live wherever in hell they've sent the jobs of hard-working Americans. Or we could slap back-breaking tariffs on the goods they manufacture in those Third-World cesspools, forcing them to try to turn a profit selling their widgets to the dollar-an-hour workers who produced them.

Finally, I, for one, am getting sick and tired of hearing how without a never-ending stream of uneducated illegals, the entire economy of the greatest industrialized nation in the history of the world would soon collapse like a fallen soufflé. Frankly, I doubt if the world has heard so much claptrap along those lines since the plantation owners wept into their mint juleps while contemplating the end of slavery.

Chapter Three

A LEGAL SYSTEM
THAT'S DOWNRIGHT CRIMINAL

11
A Capital Idea!

I would venture that the question over which Americans are most passionately divided isn't abortions or even whether or not Julia Roberts has any sex appeal, but the issue of capital punishment.

Frankly, I don't understand the position of those who are opposed to ending a life for taking a life. I mean, aside from murderers and their cohorts, criminal defense attorneys, why on earth would anybody object to society's ridding itself of its most vicious predators?

There are those people who argue that an execution is the same as a cold-blooded murder. That is such a loony contention that only a pinhead would ever suggest it. A murder, after all, involves an innocent victim; an execution doesn't.

The other major difference is that murderers are done away with as humanely as possible. That is an option that their often-tortured and mutilated victims are denied. In fact, I find it bizarre that in America there are only two groups that are provided with merciful, painless deaths — our beloved pets and our most degenerate psychopaths.

There are those, of course, who draw their inspiration from the Ten Commandments. Thou Shalt Not Kill, they repeat ad nauseam, unaware, I assume, that they are parroting a bad translation of Thou Shalt Not Murder. You don't have to be a biblical scholar to appreciate the enormous difference between those two words. It is fairly obvious that God had no qualms when it came to killing in a righteous cause. And what could possibly be more righteous than to take the life of one who has cruelly taken another's? Unlike in a war, there is no collateral damage. No innocent women and children die when a serial killer is executed. On the contrary, future atrocities are thus prevented.

Some misguided souls contend that life imprisonment is just as effective a deterrent. This contention is false for any number of reasons. The first of which is that deterring a possible crime is secondary to punishing an actual one. But, so long as a murderer is alive, there's always the chance he'll do it again — thus endangering prison guards, medical personnel, and fellow inmates. Besides, as proven not too long ago by the outgoing governor of Illinois, there's nothing to prevent a feeble-minded politician from pardoning and commuting to his heart's content.

But what about those innocent people who, through judicial error, wind up on Death Row? Would I happily see them executed? Of course not. Every effort must always be made to guarantee that justice be doled out in our courts. However, if it were left up to me, I wouldn't let a murderer off because some court of appeals decided after he was convicted that the guy's lawyer didn't measure up to Clarence Darrow, or the trial judge had neglected to tell the jury that the defendant had been spanked when he was a child — and perhaps that's why he grew up to be a mad dog.

I have heard it argued that the death penalty should be eliminated because far too many blacks and Hispanics are executed. The fact of the matter is that far too many blacks and Hispanics commit murder. To use the race card as a reason to eliminate capital punishment is sheer humbug. Study the statistics, and you'll find this to be one area in which minorities consistently over-achieve.

Finally, I resent it when people use the measure of intelligence or sanity as a reason not to execute a murderer. The well-meaning argument is that it wouldn't be fair because the defendant wouldn't have the mental capacity to assist in his own defense. Particularly where the retarded are concerned, folks like to argue that to do otherwise smacks of Hitler's Germany. To which, I reply, the Nazis eliminated such people as a matter of barbaric national policy. Their victims, no matter how kind and decent they may have been, were doomed. They were not being punished for their evil acts. As for the necessity that a defendant be able to assist in his own defense, I say the only appropriate question is whether he was capable of murdering on his own.

The way some people troop out to hold candlelight vigils every time the state executes one of these villains, you'd think they were an endangered species we were eliminating. Ah, if only they were, what a better world this would be.

Moreover, I am sick and tired of people, including members of the murder victim's own family, who self-righteously forgive the killer. The only people who have the moral authority to offer forgiveness are the victims. And I very much doubt if, given the opportunity, any of them ever would. Finally, I don't want to hear anyone insist that life in prison is worse than death. If that were truly the case, those serving life terms would all be doing the decent thing for once — imitating lemmings.

• 12 •

Being Guilty Means Never Having to Say You're Sorry

Lately, every time some scofflaw is convicted of a crime, the presiding judge and the media seem to place an enormous amount of weight on whether or not the creep was properly contrite. Am I the only person who doesn't care? If anything, I am more sympathetic towards the felon who doesn't add hypocrisy to his sins. The obvious fact is that, like a six-year-old who's caught with his hand in the cookie jar, crooks are only sorry that they've been caught.

Even worse than those who claim in court that they've seen the error of their ways are those sanctimonious phonies who suddenly make a big show of having found God in prison, hoping they'll be able to use this sudden epiphany to get time cut off their sentences. If it were up to me, I'd throw the book at them. The Good Book. Let's face it, if you can't find God before you're behind bars, you really haven't been looking. After all, it's not like He's been hiding. If I were serving on a parole board and some chucklehead tried to convince me I should grant him early release because he'd discovered religion, I'd tack on extra time for attempting to perpetrate a con game. So far as I'm concerned, if he'd truly seen the light, he'd understand better than most people why he should be punished to the full extent of the law.

I think I first developed this attitude during the aftermath of Watergate. Back in those days, I was a Democrat, and, like most of my friends, I was delighted to see Nixon leave the White House under a cloud of his own making. We were equally delighted to see his crew-cut cronies, Haldeman and Ehrlichman, crash and burn. But only I seemed to resent the fact that White House insider John Dean got so many Brownie points for essentially ratting out his chums and colleagues. I begrudgingly accept that plea bargaining is a part of modern life, but it seemed terribly inappropriate that we were bestowing heroic stature on somebody whose claim to glory was nothing more than his managing to be the first rodent off the sinking ship.

I felt that if his self-serving testimony meant lawyer Dean wasn't going to go to jail, he should at least have been shunned by society. Instead, Hollywood, well-known for its own flexible code of morality, rolled out the red carpet for Dean and the missus. The way John and Mo were feted, you'd have thought he'd done something brave and wonderful instead of having merely cut himself a deal with the prosecution, just like any other petty hood.

The only one of the lot who came out of Watergate with his dignity intact was weird G. Gordon Liddy. He didn't whine, he didn't apologize, and he served his time without trying to convince anybody that he had found either Jesus or his marbles.

In summation, I would suggest that it's only remorse if it takes place before you're arrested. After that, it's merely defense strategy.

• 13 •

Prelutsky for the Prosecution

I suppose I should be relieved. After all, this past week I was on call every day to perform jury duty, and the call never came. But, oddly enough, I'm not relieved. Instead, I'm disgruntled. It was an entire week during which I could hardly make a lunch date. The way it works, starting on Sunday night, you phone a 1-800 number, punch in a nine-digit I.D. number, and a recorded voice lets you know whether or not you have to show up at the courthouse the following morning.

Now I'll be the first to acknowledge that the present system is a major improvement over the way it used to be, when you had to actually show up and sit around a huge, noisy room most of the day, waiting to find out if you were going to be impaneled.

I'll also acknowledge that I'm not the busiest guy in the world. It's not as if I make all that many plans, and those I do make, by and large, I can make after that 6 p.m. call. In that case, you well might wonder, why do I care that next year I'll have to go through this whole rigmarole all over again? Would I so dread having to do my civic duty? Not at all. In fact, I think I'd find it an interesting experience. At least so long as they didn't make me drive all the way downtown.

The problem is that not in a million years would I ever wind up on a jury. No defense attorney in his right mind would ever let me slip by. For one thing, I wrote for several TV crime shows, ranging from "Dragnet" and "McMillan and Wife" to "Diagnosis Murder," and

I never had any qualms about doling out justice to the bad guys. In fact, on one memorable occasion, I found myself at loggerheads with "Dragnet" producer-director, Jack Webb. In an episode I wrote involving a young woman who had abandoned her newborn baby, Webb argued for an ending in which the infant would be placed in her arms and the woman would undergo a transformation from monster to Madonna in five tearjerky seconds. "Jack," I still recall saying, "she dumped her baby in a Dumpster. I'm not letting her walk. She's going to do time!" You'd have thought I was talking about an actual person. In any case, Webb backed down, and we gave her two-to-five.

Even now, when my own TV writing career is over, the only things I ever watch on the tube, aside from baseball games and old movies, are "Monk," reruns of "Columbo," and, occasionally, one of the shows making up the "Law and Order" franchise. As you may have noticed, these are all series in which nogoodniks, no matter how rich and clever they are, or how wily and underhanded their defense attorneys, get their just desserts just before the final commercial.

As if that weren't bad enough, I once wrote an article in which I confessed that one of the few things ever written by Alan Dershowitz that I accepted as gospel was his contention that more than 90% of all criminal defendants are guilty as charged.

And, finally, at the point during *voir dire* when I'd be asked if I could vote for acquittal if, in spite of a preponderance of evidence, the defense could show that the police had committed a technical error in making the arrest, I'd have to chuckle at the very notion and admit that I couldn't imagine ever doing anything that stupid.

So far as I'm concerned, if the cops make a simple human error, that in no way entitles the criminal to walk free. If, on the other hand, the cops make an intentional error, I would put the cops on trial, but I'd still be unable to grasp the logic of letting the felon scoot. I mean, short of planting evidence, employing the third degree in order to obtain a confession, or committing perjury, I fail to see how the behavior of the cops should ever affect the outcome of a criminal trial.

As you can plainly see, I simply am not cut out to be a juror. On the other hand, I think I'd make a hell of a judge.

• 14 •
The Case Against Lawyers

No sooner does one attorney attempt to ban Oreo cookies than another shmoe with a law degree is insisting that McDonald's warns its patrons that, because of the high fat and caloric content in their product, nobody should indulge more than once a week. Furthermore, he wants McDonald's, and, I assume, all other fast food chains to list the nutritional facts about their burgers, fries, and malts on the menu. Hey, I have a better idea! How about if they just replace the golden arches with a skull and crossbones?

I am not going to make an argument for junk food, except to say that the reason people buy the stuff isn't because they're so silly as to think it's the healthiest fare available. They buy it because it's cheap and it tastes pretty good.

Leave it to an attorney to insist the federal nannies step in and interfere with free enterprise. But then, lawyers, nearly always being of the liberal persuasion, believe that the bureaucrats in Washington are a lot smarter and far more trustworthy than the folks they theoretically represent.

This latest example of our wacky legal system got me to thinking. And what I'd like to know is this: How is it that in a society in which everything from toys to toasters comes with dire warnings attached, lawyers don't?

I mean, even those few simpletons who don't know that greasy meat patties aren't a health food know that much of what's wrong with America is the fault of the legal establishment. So, why is it we don't slap warning labels on these assorted ABA-approved pedophile defenders, ambulance chasers, and run-of-the-mill shysters? Just a few that readily come to mind: "Only The Other Guy's Clients Are Ever Guilty," "Will Say Anything to Get on TV," "Give Me 40% or Give Me Death," "Will Sue for Food" and "Hitler: Presumed Innocent Until Proven Guilty." The trouble is that we can't merely dismiss this gaggle of geese as a sorry bunch of clowns. Their influence is too widespread. For instance, although everybody loves to point the finger at pharmaceutical companies for the soaring costs of health care in this country, frivolous lawsuits and the subsequent expense of medical insurance are a far bigger reason.

But the true bottom-feeders of the legal profession are criminal attorneys. Under the guise of giving everyone the best defense that money can buy, these self-righteous frauds dedicate their lives to trying to spring murderers, rapists, and child molesters. They blithely defend their actions on the grounds that their concerns are with the law, not with justice. That sounds swell, but when you get past the spin, it makes them nothing more than accessories to all the crimes committed by their felonious clients. (Even Alan Dershowitz estimates that over 90% of all criminal defendants are guilty! Yet in each and every case, some mouthpiece is trying to con a judge or jury into letting them go free.)

One can only hope and pray that these pettifoggers will, one and all, ultimately face the Big Judge in the Sky — and that He, at least, will care less about legal technicalities and more about meting out divine justice. Even people who have no idea where the quotation originated have been known to agree with the suggestion that, "The first thing we do, let's kill the lawyers." But, unfortunately, as Charles Dudley Warner once observed about the weather, "Everybody talks about it, but nobody does anything about it." In any case, wouldn't it make more sense if instead of allowing some litigious lout to tie up the courts with his junk food concerns, we simply took a page out of Nancy Reagan's playbook and just said no to Happy Meals?

• 15 •
Crime and No Punishment

The other day I was talking to a friend, and, as old poops will, we tried to figure out when this country started sliding downhill. For instance, when did greed become not only acceptable, but admirable in the eyes of so many? When did we begin to accept that corporate CEOs were not only worth millions and millions of dollars in salary and stock options, but were deserving of their golden parachutes, which provided them with still more millions when their acclaimed business acumen brought their companies to the brink of bankruptcy?

When did we come to believe that self-esteem was yet another entitlement to be automatically bestowed on our young people and not something that was sought after and earned? At what point did we decide that the kids were supposed to be treated the way monarchies treat their royals? The bedroom of a typical middle class kid looks like a Toys 'R' Us warehouse. Sneakers, which used to be the cheapest footwear this side of socks, now cost an arm and a leg. And parents pay the freight because no kid will be seen in public if Kobe or Shaq doesn't have his name smeared on his shoes. You might think that just out of sheer gratitude, the young sprouts would at least mow the lawn or take out the trash once in a while. But, as you may have noticed, William and Andrew don't do chores around Buckingham, either.

My friend suspected the decline of American civilization began with Nixon and Watergate. He felt it made us cynical about politics and politicians in a way we'd never been before. I disagreed. I felt that Nixon and his scandal created a sea change, but mainly in the way the media operated in this country. Suddenly, journalism became appealing to a certain besotted segment of the youthful population. The kids could picture themselves as the next Woodward or Bernstein, getting rich and famous while bringing down the high and mighty.

I happen to think that the country's general decline began in the 1960s. For the first time in history, youngsters were being held up as the moral, behavioral, and cultural arbiters of the nation. Parents were looking to their children as role models. Forty-year-olds were suddenly trying to dress, think, and even wear their hair like teenagers.

The combination of drugs, free sex, and irresponsible parents made it inevitable that an entire generation grew up despising not only their own parents and the parents of their friends, but all authority figures. They called cops "pigs," and they spit on soldiers. The only adults they had any use for were those whom they regarded as rebels, mainly cynical poseurs who made a handsome living thumbing their noses at what passed for polite society — people like Hunter S. Thompson, Tom Hayden, Jane Fonda, and safely tenured liberal arts professors.

Please understand that I had my own share of distaste for authority figures. I still do. They just don't happen to be the same ones that Ward Churchill, Cindy Sheehan, and Al Franken have. Whereas the perpetually infantile vent their spleen on such folks as Bush, Cheney, Rumsfeld, Rice, and Scalia, I reserve my contempt for the likes of Michael Moore, John Kerry, Ariana Huffington, Susan Estrich, Jesse Jackson, and Deborah Robinson.

You're probably wondering who this Ms. Robinson could be that she should find herself lumped in such undistinguished company. She happens to be the U.S. magistrate who recently fined former national security adviser Sandy Berger $50,000 for stealing classified documents from the National Archives.

While Judge Robinson thought she was being quite stern, I saw it as just one more muddleheaded miscarriage of justice. She was patting herself on the back because the prosecution was only recommending a fine of $10,000. (You have to wonder why the government lawyers even bothered taking the matter to court and didn't simply have Mr. Berger mail a check to traffic court.)

"The court finds the $10,000 fine inadequate because it doesn't reflect the seriousness of the offense," Judge Robinson declared. But $50,000, and no jail time, does?! Hell, baseball players get fined that much for accidentally bumping an umpire while arguing a close play at second base.

You are probably wondering why I find the judge more contemptible than the defendant. It's because Mr. Berger has provided me with several yocks along the way. First he had me giggling when he committed the crime by shoving those documents down the front of his pants. I happen to be a sucker for physical comedy. What's more, I'm in awe of his courage; the man is apparently fearless, at least when it comes to paper cuts.

Then, he had me laughing out loud when he said, after being found out, that he had simply misplaced the papers. Misplaced them in his boxer shorts? Boy, talk about being absentminded!

Even after admitting that he had destroyed three of the five documents by cutting them up with scissors, he called it an honest mistake. Man, you can't write funnier stuff than that.

But it was at his hearing that Sandy "Always Leave Them Laughing" Berger had me rolling on the floor. "I let considerations of personal convenience override clear rules of handling classified material, but I believe this lapse, serious as it is, does not reflect the character of myself." The character of myself?! Who taught this man to speak? Elmer Fudd?

"In this case, I failed," he said. "I will not again." Considering he got off with a slap on the wrist, I would say that it was not he, but Judge Robinson, who failed in this case.

Nevertheless, I, for one, am taking him at his word. And, so, if he ever shows up at my front door, I'm hiding the good silver. After all, next time he might be wearing reinforced jockey shorts.

• 16 •
Those Poor, Poor Perverts

I can nearly, but not quite, understand why some people object to capital punishment. After all, if they're unaware that Thou Shall Not Kill is a bad translation of Thou Shall Not Murder, you can see where they might wind up believing that the execution of a serial killer is as sinful as the original crime. Of course I happen to think that, at this late date, there's no excuse for a grown-up not having bothered to find out what the sixth commandment actually says. That's especially the case if he's going to carry on as if he has dibs on the moral high ground and accuse those who disagree with him of being bloodthirsty thugs.

That said, what I can't begin to fathom are the people who seem to have the same tender feelings for sexual predators that the rest of us have for our pets. Unfortunately, these aren't the same mushy-headed simpletons holding candlelight vigils outside San Quentin. Instead, they're judges and legislators.

Each time I hear any of these people discuss how many feet away from a school playground or a park some pedophile should be allowed to live, I'm reminded of those nuts in the Middle Ages who whiled away their days arguing over how many angels could dance on the head of a pin. It's as if I had just awakened in Oz to discover that my farmhouse had landed smack dab on top of a witch named Common Sense.

For what reason would any sane society ever release such a person from jail? The notion that kids are safe if the creep lives 2,000 feet away from where they play is perfectly loony. What about the

kids walking to and from those parks and playgrounds? Are we supposed to take the freak's word that he'll behave himself? If so, why
not release all the bank robbers, making certain that none of them
lives closer than two blocks away from the nearest branch of First
National? I can absolutely guarantee you that robbers can control
their desire to knock over a bank a heck of a lot better than perverts
can be counted on to control their degenerate urges.

Only judges and lawmakers seem happy to ignore the rates of
recidivism among rapists and pedophiles. Is there anyone else, aside
from defense attorneys, who would argue that a man who's raped a
six-year-old child deserves a second chance?

Whenever I read about the problems of resettling these creeps
and then trying to keep track of them until the day they die, I can
only shake my head. Why should anyone be able to destroy the life
of a child and the child's family and ever be allowed to see the light
of day again? So far as I'm concerned, the only place they belong
isn't 700 yards from the nearest see-saw, but in a dungeon or in
Hell. Next best would be having them move in with a politician or a
judge.

• 17 •

Roe V. Wade V. Prelutsky

Sometimes, I get the idea that I'm the only person in America who can clearly see both sides of the abortion issue. Or, to put it another way, I think the zealots on both sides of the controversy should be hosed down until they come to their senses.

Frankly, I wish that a woman's right to have an abortion had never become a national issue and that the Supreme Court had kept its nose out of it. But the justices of the Supreme Court long ago gave up even the pretense of merely interpreting the Constitution in favor of creating legislation. And who can blame them? In Hollywood, after all, everybody wants to direct. In Washington, everybody wants to make laws. In both cases, it's the natural human inclination to boss people around.

It has become such a major and divisive issue that I sometimes think that if liberals didn't have their pro-abortion platform to rally around, the Democrats would go the way of the Whigs and the Bull Moose.

I can understand why the right to legal abortions is so important to so many women. The nightmarish memories of backroom operations performed by butchers remain too vivid to be forgotten. As a man, I am convinced that abortions would be readily available in all 50 states if men were the ones who got pregnant.

However, I can also understand why some people regard abortions as immoral. Where the so-called pro-lifers go wrong is in equating abortion with cold-blooded murder. If that were truly the case, people who killed abortionists would be heroes, not lunatics, and people who did not kill abortionists would be cowards.

Here, then, is my own take on the subject: I think the voters in each state should decide the law. I believe that no minor should have one performed without parental consent; it is bizarre to imagine that a teenager should require a parent's consent to have a tooth removed, but not a fetus. I think if an unmarried woman has the sole authority to abort or not to abort, she then has no right to demand child support of her sex partner. However, I would have a siring tax. Society should not do anything to encourage illegitimacy, either by providing the mother with an annuity or allowing the father a free ride.

As people once argued over how many angels could dance on the head of a pin, they now argue over when a fetus becomes a human being. At one extreme, we have Norman Mailer, who regards masturbation as immoral because he holds his sperm in such high regard. Then we have those at the other end of the spectrum, who argue that so long as the fetus is in the womb, abortion is a viable option. So far as they're concerned, the difference between a perfectly legal medical procedure and murder can be a matter of minutes.

For my part, the pro-abortion crowd surrenders the moral high ground every time it insists that a woman has an inalienable right to do what she will with her own body, and that removing a fetus is the same as removing a wart. No wart, these feminists should be reminded, ever became a living, breathing child. Nobody ever celebrated the announcement that a wife, daughter, sister, niece, or friend had just discovered she had a wart. Nobody ever painted a room pink, bought out a toy store, and threw a party in anticipation of a wart.

And nobody ever named a wart "Junior."

• 18 •

Toot, Toot, Tookie, Goodbye

Let me begin by stating that I am in favor of capital punishment. I don't view it as a deterrent, understand, I consider it the only appropriate punishment for cold-blooded murder. Actually, I have only two objections to it. The first is that the killer with more than one murder to his credit can only be executed the one time. Next, I resent the fact that no matter how much he may have tortured his victims, society has seen fit to send him off as painlessly as possible. I find it bizarre that in a country where mercy killings are illegal even for the terminally ill, only vicious psychopaths and our beloved pets are guaranteed a merciful death.

That brings me to the recently departed Stanley Williams, better known as Tookie. Speaking of which, I, for one, resent that the media — as if beholden to his defense team — kept calling this stone-cold killer Tookie, as if he were some child's teddy bear.

Stanley Williams used a shotgun to blow the heads off four people. That's some teddy bear.

I knew that Williams was being held up as a reformed character because he supposedly used his influence to steer young people away from gangs. Considering the escalating number of gang-related murders, it seems that Mr. Williams, who was the founding father of the Crips, was a lot better at getting kids into gangs than out of them.

Although intellectually I can grasp the point of view of those morally opposed to capital punishment, emotionally I am unable to fathom how they can congregate outside prisons and hold candlelight vigils for mass murderers. Wouldn't their time be better spent visiting the burial sites of the victims and leaving flowers instead of candle wax behind?

There are those who claim that Williams, who never voiced remorse for his crimes, had found redemption behind bars. They point out that he had even written a children's book. Never having had occasion to read it, it took Michael Medved to point out that Williams had dedicated it to Nelson Mandela. To Nelson Mandela, that is, along with a slew of cop killers!

Some of his fans argue that Williams, having spent over a quarter of a century in prison, was a totally different person than the guy who'd been convicted. Well, it's true that he hadn't shotgunned anybody to death in all that time. But I happen to believe it's far more relevant that his victims had been deprived of a cumulative hundred years of life by this brute, and that doesn't even begin to approach what their friends and families lost.

Claiming that it was immoral, after all these years of incarceration, to execute Williams makes as much sense as appearing as amicus curiae on behalf of the man who murders his parents and then pleads for mercy as an orphan. If Williams and his lawyers hadn't filed appeal after appeal, he would have been executed in a far more timely fashion.

To me, the only amusing aspect of this entire matter is that the man was constantly being identified as a Nobel Prize nominee. Sometimes he was a nominee for literature, other times for peace. For all I know, he may have been nominated for both. He may even have been nominated for medicine, physics, and economics. The truth of the matter is that anybody can nominate anyone for a Nobel prize. In fact, considering that the likes of Le Duc Tho, Kofi Annan, Jimmy Carter, and his friend Yasser Arafat have actually been honorees, you can see that not only can absolutely any shmoe be nominated, he can even win.

Quite frankly, I was surprised that Gov. Schwarzenegger allowed the execution to take place. With all the campaigning on behalf of Williams by the Hollywood elite, I fully expected him to capitulate.

I'm glad my instincts were wrong. It took gumption for Schwarzenegger to do the right thing. The Terminator may be gone, but the Exterminator is alive and well and taking care of business in Sacramento.

Hasta la vista, Tookie.

CHAPTER FOUR

Q: WHAT DO ISLAM AND
THE BUBONIC PLAGUE
HAVE IN COMMON?
A: JUST ABOUT EVERYTHING.

• 19 •
Allah Be Appraised!

Although I have never claimed to be as politically correct as, say, *The New York Times,* I like to think of myself as a reasonably open-minded fellow where people who are different from me are concerned. And, inasmuch as most people are very different from me — and glad of it — I get a lot of practice. Furthermore, I have always contended that bigots are just plain lazy, and that if you just take the trouble to know people as individuals, almost invariably you will discover better reasons to despise them other than their race, religion, or sexual proclivity.

So, please believe me when I swear I'm convinced the great majority of American Muslims mean it when they say they're loyal to this country. What I refuse to accept for a single second is their contention that Osama bin Laden is an aberration, an unholy defiler of the tenets of their peace-loving religion. As people used to say, tell it to the Marines.

No, I have not read the Qur'an. And while I have heard highly inflammatory excerpts from those who have read the holy book, I'm aware that Satan can quote or even misquote scripture to his own purpose. Another ancient adage, however, states that the proof is in the pudding. In the case of Islam, I would suggest that the pudding is to be found in every nation where Muslims hold the reins. Or, perhaps, one should say, the whip.

Can it be mere coincidence that, although democracy has flourished in nations that are predominantly Protestant, Catholic, Hindu, Jewish, Shinto, Buddhist, Lutheran, and Anglican, it never takes root where Muhammad's word is law? Can it be mere happenstance that wherever you look in the Muslim world, from Sudan to Syria, from Iraq to Iran, from Libya to Saudi Arabia, wherever Islam holds sway you will find one totalitarian state after another? True, you will find a variety of national leaders, including oil-rich sheiks, fanatical ayatollahs and run-of-the-mill tyrants like Qaddafi, Assad and Mahmoud Ahmadinejad, but one and all could dine comfortably with a Russian czar or a Chicago gangster.

For an allegedly peaceful religion, isn't it remarkable that wherever Islam gains a stranglehold, you will find the nightmare of slavery, genocide, and female stoning and mutilation the norm?

I have heard folks say that the historical reason for all this is that, of all the founders of the major religions, only Muhammad was a warrior. Although a merchant by trade, he led his followers in the bloody conquest of Mecca. So perhaps the die was cast thirteen centuries ago. Hell, for all I know, maybe it goes back to climate. I know I'm a perfect grouch when the temperature goes through the roof and the air conditioning conks out. Maybe it has something to do with too much sand in one's diet. Or perhaps sharing one's life with camels, notoriously nasty beasts, is the reason behind the cult of death that celebrates suicide bombings throughout the Arab world.

To tell you the truth, when I first heard tell of the awards that supposedly awaited Islamic martyrs, even I began to see the attraction. I mean, on the face of it, moving from Jenin, say, to Paradise sounds like an awfully good deal. Toss in six dozen beautiful virgins, and what healthy, red-blooded Palestinian wouldn't gladly blow himself to Kingdom Come? The problem, of course, is that, like most youngsters, they never bother thinking things through. For instance, in the natural course of events, what the young fool will soon have on his hands are six dozen ex-virgins. And if he thinks he has it bad now, just wait until he winds up spending eternity with

72 women who while away each and every day complaining that he's always leaving his burnoose on the floor, doesn't help out with the kids, and never takes them dancing.

• 20 •
Islam Is a Riot

The best thing about the rioting in France is that it proves once and for all that pandering to Islamists is always a bad idea. Even when you provide them with all the perks available to sluggards in a socialist society, it's no guarantee they won't turn right around and bite the hand that feeds them. So, just in case anybody ever asks you to name the biggest difference between a French Muslim and a French poodle, you now know the answer.

France made the mistake of throwing open its doors forty years ago to cheap Arab and African workers, and came to discover, to its dismay, that the children and grandchildren of those original immigrants don't care for the French any more than the rest of us do.

There are those who believe that the rioting is the result of the French failing to assimilate Muslims into their society. Far be it from me to defend France, something you may have noticed over the past century the French, themselves, are extremely reluctant to do. However, you might as well condemn Old MacDonald for not assimilating with his farm animals. It's not French snobbery that isolates the Muslims or creates their embarrassingly high rate of unemployment. The fact of the matter is that their young men are too spoiled and too lazy to do manual labor, and too ignorant and ill-educated to do anything else. Combine a welfare state that provides them with food and lodging with a vulgar religion that condemns all nonbelievers as infidels, and you have gasoline just waiting for a lighted match.

Most liberal pundits, I've found, justify riots, blaming society at large for its marauders. I, on the other hand, am not so easily hood-winked. Check out the photos of every riot you've ever seen, and you will discover that it's the very same riff-raff in every mob, no matter where the vandalism takes place. Remove the sixteen- to twenty-five-year-old male punks from the pictures and you'd be left with a lot of lampposts and telephone poles minding their own business.

Whether it's the Rodney King mob burning down stores in L.A., the PLO bums throwing stones in Jenin, or the lay-abouts in Paris, they're exactly the same as the punks in America who run amok every time their home team either wins or loses a Super Bowl or an NBA title. There is a reason why you rarely see anybody over the age of 30 out in the streets. Could it be that only youngsters are ever oppressed or downtrodden? Hardly. It's because even their own parents know that the young hoodlums would be just as likely to stone them as to stone the cops; far likelier, in fact, because their folks are less likely to be armed and dangerous.

It's no secret that testosterone-driven young males enjoy busting windows, spray-painting graffiti, and starting fires. Unfortunately, just as with certain parents who are in denial when it comes to the antics of their bratty children, social workers, members of the liberal media, and other assorted pacifists habitually blame riots on capital-ism, Western imperialism, oil companies, and, for all I know, prema-ture potty training.

Frankly, what I most fear is that in a world in which multicultur-alists, including even President Bush and Secretary of State Rice, feel obliged to bow and scrape to Muslims in a world so overflowing with infantile feel-good rhetoric about the joys of Islam, that it will eventually and inevitably give rise to fascism.

Each time I hear people defending Islam, pretending that it's merely another humanistic faith like Christianity, Judaism and

Buddhism, I wonder if they would have insisted that National Socialism was just another political party, and that being a Nazi was no different from being a Republican or a Democrat.

I worry that in a world filled with folks lying about the emperor, it will finally take a Hitler to point out he's as naked as a jaybird.

Frankly, I'm sick and tired of hearing people parroting the lie that Islam is a religion of peace. I suppose so long as you're willing to set aside your bible and pick up the Koran and start kneeling to Mecca, they'll let you live in peace; unless, of course, you belong to a different sect. In which case, in the name of the great and merciful Allah, they'd have no choice but to lop your head off.

Of course American Muslims aren't like the butchers and suicide bombers who murder in the name of their religion, or so we're told. But just how would we know that to be true? What we do know is that even after 9/11, until the F.B.I. put a stop to it, many of them were funneling funds to Al Qaeda.

Before I'm persuaded that there's a real difference between our Muslims and those other ones, the faithful in the U.S. will have to first stop whining about racial profiling; their young people will have to start enlisting in the armed services; and they'll have to begin condemning their co-religionists loudly and often. For openers, it would be a nice gesture if they passed the hat around the old mosque and then announced they'd come up with a multi-million dollar reward for Osama bin Laden, dead or alive.

As for the rest of us, it's high time we stopped trying to come up with highfalutin' excuses for murderous mobs.

The answer, nearly always, to why young people riot is simple. It's fun.

• 21 •
A Modest Proposal

Only the hopelessly naïve, the same fools who believed Hitler was going to be satisfied with merely gobbling up the Sudetenland, actually believe that the Islamic fascists would all become saints and shepherds if only the U.S. got out of Iraq or out of the Middle East altogether.

If that were all it took, life would be a bowl of cherries. Heck, I'd even be happy to move all the Jews out of Israel and into one of our northern states. If they could turn the desert into a garden, think what they could do with North Dakota. At the very least, Bismarck would have first-rate hospitals, a terrific university, a hell of a state National Guard, more entrepreneurs than the Silicon Valley, and a world class symphony orchestra.

In the meantime, under Palestinian stewardship, the land formerly known as Israel would revert to sand and rubble. And the Muslims could get back to doing what they do best, namely, slaughtering one another.

Unfortunately, life's never that simple. The Muslims don't hate us because we're in Iraq, but because we exist. They hate us because we're everything they are not — advanced technologically, democratic, powerful, and Judeo-Christian. We don't subjugate and mutilate our women, we don't behead our enemies, and our young men don't blow themselves up in the hope of spending eternity in a celestial brothel.

They despise our music, our movies, our tattoos and body-piercing, our TV shows, and even the way we dress. Okay, there's something to be said for their side, I'll grant you, but not much.

If all the Muslims around the world would move back to the backwaters from whence they came, back to the good old days of the ninth century, I, for one, would happily bid them *adieu*. But, instead, they're busy causing misery and havoc all over the place — butchering civilians in Bali, London, Madrid, the Philippines, South Africa, New York, the Sudan — all in the name of Allah.

I understand I am tarring people who have never lifted a hand in anger, people who are presumably disgusted by the activities of their co-religionists. But that's not good enough. By and large, even here in America, their silence is deafening. One doesn't hear their religious leaders condemning the terrorists; at most, you hear them whining about racial profiling. Odd that the same religion that put a $2 million price on the head of novelist Salman Rushdie hasn't seen fit to place a reward of even a plugged nickel on the head of Osama bin Laden.

Fourteen hundred years ago, Muhammad, founder of Islam, converted at the point of a sword, and I'm afraid that his followers got the message. Islam, in spite of modern-day spin, does not mean peace. The word actually translates to submission or surrender.

Assuming there are decent Muslims in the world, people who are not a disgrace to the human race, I have a suggestion to offer. Rather than be shamed every hour of every day by the revolting barbarism of your fellow Islamics, why not forsake Muhammad for a religious leader who not only preached, but practiced, kindness, charity, and love? Why not do unto others as you would have others do unto you, and convert...to Christianity?

• 22 •

How to Make Hitler Look Good

Even though I may not look it, I am essentially a pretty happy guy. Like most people my age, I get out of sorts when I consider the steady decline of art, culture, and baseball. But so long as nobody puts a gun to my head and makes me listen to hip hop, and so long as I don't have to watch MTV or suffer through yet another Jim Carrey movie, I don't let myself get too perturbed by current trends. I don't even object to the mudslinging one associates with presidential campaigns. I just remind myself that nobody ever got to sling mud at Joseph Stalin or Saddam Hussein.

Two of the few things that I do find truly depressing are Islamic fanatics and those Americans on the radical left who defend their atrocities. I can't be the only person who finds it peculiar that the very same people who break out in a cold sweat over the slightest overlap of church and state in the U.S., who despise evangelical Christians and distrust orthodox Jews, have no problem arguing on behalf of people who saw the heads off civilian hostages, who treat their women like chattel, and who will happily conduct bloodbaths over a few cartoons.

What I find most disconcerting about these Muslims is that they almost manage to make the Nazis look normal by comparison. This is not to suggest that Hitler and his butchers weren't abominable. Hitler was an evil lunatic who wished to wage war on mankind and thus turn *"Deutschland uber alles"* into more than a catchy slogan. But at least the world he set out to conquer was the world of the 20th century. You have only to look at Berchtesgaden, his palace in the mountains, to understand that the man loved excess. He may have been a vegetarian, but the little bastard was a hedonist at heart.

Der fuhrer and his cohorts appreciated art and music, architecture and film, beautiful women and schnapps. The only thing that makes the Nazis worse than the barbaric Islamics is that, being technologically advanced, they were more efficient killers.

The world of the mullahs is the world of the Dark Ages. It is an ugly place and it smells like a sewer. It is as enlightened as a cesspool. It turns its back on life and it celebrates death. Its heroes are suicide bombers. Its motto is, better a dead martyr than a living child. Who would choose to live in such a world? Only the hopelessly insane.

I say, whatever it costs to defeat this plague is well worth the price, just as the costs were justified to rid the world of the Third Reich.

At times, I confess, I get downhearted because it seems such an impossible task. The Muslim terrorists, after all, seem to be everywhere in the world, blowing up buildings, blowing up people. We bring down Saddam Hussein as we brought down Hitler, but still the fighting rages on in Iraq. How can we hope to defeat people who aren't merely fighting for a leader or a nation, but because of their religion, because Muhammad gave them their marching orders fourteen hundred years ago?

Well, in spite of all that, I find reasons to be hopeful. For instance, think about the French Revolution. One day, the French were ruled by a despotic king; the next day, *"Voila!"* they weren't.

One day, here in America, we had slavery; the next day, after two hundred years, we didn't.

One day, Italy was being bossed around by a two-bit thug named Mussolini; the next day, he was in the town square, hanging upside down like a side of beef.

One day, the Soviet Union had a few hundred million Eastern

Europeans under its brutal thumb; the next day it barely had a thumb.

But even more to the point, consider Japan. The Japanese who invaded China, Korea, Shanghai, and Manchuria and bombed the hell out of the American fleet at Pearl Harbor, thought they were on a holy mission on behalf of their emperor. Think of it as a jihad with a sake chaser.

Emperor Hirohito was more than a national leader; he was a god. He was as distant and mysterious as the great and powerful Wizard of Oz. When he went on the radio in 1945, after Hiroshima and Nagasaki, to announce to the nation that the war was over and that they had lost, his countrymen didn't know what to make of it. They had never heard his voice. Gods, for god's sake, don't talk on the radio.

Because Hirohito was regarded as a deity, dying on his behalf had been regarded as a holy act. The Japanese, as you may recall, had had their own version of suicide bombers; they were called Kamikazes. They were pilots whose sole mission was to fly their explosive-laden Zeros directly into allied battleships and destroyers. Next stop, they were told: Paradise. Sound vaguely familiar?

So ingrained in the Japanese was blind devotion to their emperor that, long after the war was over, isolated soldiers were found on South Pacific islands still defending their turf. They simply hadn't heard God on the short-wave.

Who would have ever guessed that in no time at all, Japan would not only be a peace-loving democracy, but that its citizens would feel as free as the English to gossip about the royal family, and would revere baseball players above all other mortals?

In other words, what so often seems impossible to imagine only means that imagination is often lacking.

From all this, I find hope that the Islamic necrophiliacs will go the way of the Visigoths and the Huns, Napoleon and the Nazis.

I believe that we will destroy them because, having vowed to destroy all of us — even those who speak on their behalf — they really leave us no choice in the matter.

I am curious about one thing, though. When Arab terrorists speak about martyring themselves so that they can go directly to Paradise, is their vision of the place as desolate and as gruesome as the world they're trying to foist on the rest of us?

Does it at least have indoor plumbing?

• 23 •

Sandbox Sermons

Quite often when people are in a mood to insult world leaders, they'll accuse them of behaving like children. To which I say, I only wish it were so.

The fact of the matter is that most kids have a very moral take on things. Because they are small and weak, their very survival requires total concentration and a very clear focus. They have a heightened sense of good and bad because their lives consist of inevitable repercussions. Whereas most adults can get away with stuff so long as cops and the IRS don't find out about it, kids are nearly always under extremely close scrutiny. That's why children will often be heard to say, "That's not fair" or "You cheated" or "It's my turn." They make concise and immediate moral judgments that would make a Jesuit's head spin. It is behavior not much favored by grownups, most of whom exist in a world of moral ambiguity; after a certain age, black and white disappears in a morass of gray.

For instance, adults recognize that illegal immigration is an enormous problem in America. Even before 9/11, it was a major headache. Millions of Hispanics crossing our border were adding a terrible burden to our schools, our hospitals, and, yes, our prisons. States such as California, Texas, and Arizona were being overrun by these invaders whose very first act in their new country was to break the law!

When some people dared to state concern, their voices were drowned out by the Hispanic politicians looking to tie up blocs of votes and the Catholic hierarchy looking to fill up empty pews.

Suggest that the country didn't really need ten million unskilled laborers and you were denounced as a racist. Suggest that Americans would bus tables and pick lettuce if the price were right and you were flogged as an enemy of free enterprise.

I have argued long and hard that most Americans would rather pay an extra five cents for a head of lettuce than subsidize the farm industry with illegal laborers. But the politicians continue to champion the bracero program as if it were the answer to a prayer. And I suppose it is if you're running for office, own a 10,000 acre farm in the Imperial Valley, or head up a diocese.

Of course if I were a kid, I could have saved my breath. Explain to a seven-year-old that there are millions of people all over the world, their names on official lists, waiting their turn to enter America legally, and he'd sum up the illegal alien problem with a terse, "No fair taking cuts!"

Or consider our current problem with Iraq. As I write this, the war has been going on for just a little while. Thus far, Saddam Hussein hasn't unleashed any toxic chemicals on allied forces. He has, however, executed POWs on TV, he has stashed weapons in hospitals and day care centers, he has forced his own citizens to provide cover for his soldiers, he has fired missiles into Kuwait, and he has had his troops show the white flag and then open fire on Americans and Brits. But, allow me to make a long-overdue confession: It never made much difference to me if Hussein had weapons of mass destruction. For my part, I didn't even require proof positive that he played an active role in the 9/11 atrocities. I was satisfied that he funded suicide bombers and that he gassed Kurds, and that was good enough — or bad enough — for me.

I'm even willing to go on record to state that if the only thing he'd done over the past twenty-five years was to torture and murder his fellow Iraqis, I'd be happy to see my tax dollars go to exterminating the Butcher of Baghdad.

I realize that it is anathematic for many Americans to even consider waging war against a country that hasn't bombed Pearl Harbor. But, frankly, I don't know why. These people go ballistic when they hear of a few Iraqis killed inadvertently by allied soldiers, but when it comes to Hussein's reign of terror that victimized tens of thousands of those same Iraqis, they merely stifle a yawn and say something in French.

To all of them, I pose a single question: If Hitler hadn't invaded other countries, should the world have given him carte blanche to do whatever he wished in Germany?

Turning the clock back seventy years, would the same people who are currently carrying placards in the streets equating Bush with Hitler have campaigned against allied intervention so long as der Fuhrer only tortured and gassed Jews, gays, Gypsies, Catholics, Socialists, dissidents, and the infirm, who were unfortunate enough to be German?

It seems so obvious to me that it is not merely weapons of mass destruction that should inflame our sense of injustice, it is also evil of massive proportion.

The morally vapid will continue to put their misguided faith in an organization as toothless and craven as the U.N., just as their equally naïve grandparents put theirs in the League of Nations. Someone once said that a camel was a horse put together by a committee. In similar fashion, the specialty of world peace organizations is to make grand pronouncements of irresolute resolutions. Whether it was dealing with Italy, Germany, and Japan in the 1930s or Iraq, North Korea, and Islamic terrorists today, the professional peacemakers can always be counted on to shake a stern finger, go "tsk-tsk," and then call for a time-out.

Once you get past Russia's oil contracts and France's envy and hatred of the United States, there's nothing very complicated about dealing with the Saddam Husseins of the world. And once again, you can find the appropriate response in the sandboxes of our land. For, every third grader in America knows that schoolyard bullies never stop bullying until some kid with a bit of gumption gets fed up at long last and punches the little brat in the nose.

• 24 •
French-Fried Politics

To me, the worst thing about Muslims, aside from their longing to be returned to the good old days of the eighth century, and to drag the rest of us, kicking and screaming, along with them, is the fact that far too many politically correct imbeciles feel compelled to accommodate them and to find rationales for their violence. Two such enablers who come to mind, I'm sad to say, are George W. Bush and Condoleezza Rice. Both have promoted the lie that Islam is a religion of peace and good will. Perhaps in some parallel universe where day is night, up is down, and love is hate, it is so. But here on planet Earth, Islam is a religion whose mullahs preach sermons of death to the infidels. And just in case you haven't noticed, that includes everybody who doesn't spend several minutes every day bowing down to Mecca.

Yet we have the spectacle of American and European leftists arguing in the defense of people who regard suicide bombings of school buses as a legitimate form of guerrilla warfare; who speak up on behalf of men who treat their wives and daughters as chattel; and who refer to those butchers who hack the heads off innocent civilians as freedom fighters.

The French assumed that because they had built Iraq's nuclear reactor, played a leading role in Hussein's oil-for-food scam, and vigorously opposed U.S. intervention in Iraq, they were safely shielded from Islamic high jinks. As recent events have proven, nobody is safe from their insanity. And considering what has taken place in

Iran, Iraq, Kuwait, Indonesia, Sudan, and other predominantly Islamic countries, that definitely includes their fellow Muslims.

In a brilliant tongue-in-cheek essay, Joseph Farah wondered if the intifada currently taking place in France would cause Jacques Chirac and his political cronies to resolve their problem with Islamic fanatics in the same fashion they have long argued that Israel should solve hers; namely, by turning over large parcels of territory so that the bloodthirsty fanatics can have their own sovereign nation.

Knowing the French as we all do, I suspect that it is a solution they will enthusiastically support. However, the territory wouldn't be carved out of Nice or Marseilles or — mon dieu! — certainly not Paris. Instead, in typically French style, it would be Luxembourg, Liechtenstein or perhaps, once again, Czechoslovakia.

CHAPTER FIVE

FLOTSAM AND JETSAM

• 25 •
Lions And Tigers and Reds...
Oh, My!

In Ann Coulter's book, *Treason,* she holds the Democrats responsible for underestimating, intentionally or unintentionally, the danger posed by the late, unlamented, Soviet Union. However, she tends to downplay the role played by the Republicans.

In the '40s and '50s, far too many people on the Right were basing their careers solely on being anti-Communist. Which might have been okay, except for the fact that they all looked like B-movie villains! If a call had come in to Central Casting from a producer needing a few extras for a movie he was making about the American Bund, the next morning five shmoes who looked exactly like Joe McCarthy, Roy Cohn, Richard Nixon, Karl Mundt, and J. Parnell Thomas would have shown up on the set.

Let's face it — guys like Nixon and McCarthy already looked like nasty caricatures even before Herblock put charcoal pencil to paper.

It didn't help that these guys spent way too much time sniffing out Communists in Hollywood. That's not to say there weren't a lot of them working at the studios in those days, or that some of them weren't sending tithes to Moscow, but it was obvious that the members of HUAC weren't tracking down dangerous characters. What they were hunting for was headlines.

By concentrating on people such as Larry Parks and Gale Sondergaard, they managed to trivialize the evil inherent in Soviet Communism. After all, if the worst thing Americans had to fear was yet another sequel to *The Jolson Story* or that Ms. Sondergaard would continue to chew up the scenery at Paramount, the Red Menace was clearly no big deal.

But the part that personal appearance played in the public perception can't be ignored. The Rosenbergs, for instance, as secret Soviet files later confirmed, were spies and traitors. But they didn't look the way enemy agents looked in the movies. They weren't smooth, polished, and sophisticated, like Conrad Veidt and Otto Kruger. Instead, they looked like your shloompy Uncle Julius and Aunt Ethel. Who could picture them sending A-bomb secrets to the Soviet Union? A nice pumpernickel, maybe, but atomic secrets? Never!

Or take the case of Alger Hiss. Mr. Hiss was a tall, slim, dapper, career diplomat. The man who accused him of being one of Stalin's secret weapons in the U.S. State Department was a fat man named Whitaker Chambers, who looked like an unmade bed. In a movie, Cary Grant would have been cast as Hiss; Sydney Greenstreet would have been Chambers. No contest. The only problem, of course, is that, as is often the case, appearances were deceiving. Chambers was telling the truth, while Hiss was committing perjury. It seems that Hiss' misguided idealism had placed him right in the pocket of Joseph Stalin; he took his marching orders directly from the Politburo. But he looked so good that, to this day, many people on the Left are still convinced that he was the innocent victim of a witch hunt.

So, the fault, whether or not Ms. Coulter agrees, was to be found on both sides of America's internal Cold War. The liberal dupes were so beguiled by Stalin — "Uncle Joe," as they liked to call him — that anything and anybody they perceived to be his foe was automatically a Fascist and, therefore, their sworn enemy.

Right up to the time of his recent death, Elia Kazan's enemies claimed they reviled him because he had named names. How ridiculous is that? Hollywood, as we all know, is a community renowned for its hypocrisy and its absolute lack of common decency. The sin in their eyes wasn't that Kazan had ratted on his ex-friends, but that his ex-friends happened to be Communists. Had they been Fascists or even garden variety reactionaries, this same crowd would have erected a statue in Kazan's honor at the corner of Hollywood and Vine.

But the Right was not blameless. The first of their two major flaws was that they focused their attention on what were then called "pinkos" and "fellow travelers" by Americans, and "useful idiots" by the Russkies. That was a terribly misguided case of not seeing the forest for the trees. Or, in this instance, hardly trees, more like ants. In retrospect, for all their ranting and flag waving and picketing the- aters showing movies starring people like Kim Hunter and John Garfield, they failed to grasp the nature or even the identity of the true enemy.

Then, to compound that profound error of judgment, they cast a bunch of Neanderthals who looked and behaved like fugitives from a lynch mob in the lead roles.

Fortunately, in the final reel we got our happy ending when the cavalry, in the form of co-stars Ronald Reagan and Mikhail Gorbachev, rode in and saved the day.

· 26 ·

Bargain-Rate Bribes

As Shakespeare once observed, more or less, who steals my purse steals trash, blah blah blah, but he that filches from me my good name, yada yada yada, makes me poor indeed.

Well, the Bard of Avon and the Burt of North Hills are in total agreement regarding the importance of one's reputation, although I do think he went slightly overboard with that trash line. I can only assume the Bard never had his wallet lifted, and then had to go about replacing his driver's license and all those Visa, MasterCard, Social Security, Medicare, and Auto Club cards.

I have no reason to think that Bill and I are the only people who, like Cyrano de Bergerac, regard our reputations as white plumes well worth defending, even at the point of a sword. So, tell me, how is it that so many politicians, no matter their party, place so little value on their own?

I was just a kid when one of Eisenhower's closest associates, Sherman Adams, saw his own career scuttled when it came out that he'd accepted a vicuna coat from someone who wanted access to the White House.

It wasn't too many years later that Lyndon Johnson's protégé, Bobby Baker, saw his future turn to ashes when he accepted a stereo set from somebody whose name wasn't Santa Claus.

These days, we see the folks up on Capitol Hill running around in a panic, trying to pass measures to deal with ethics violations. And just what are we talking about? What is it that has these congressmen and senators in such a tizzy? What is it they have to vow never to do again? Hold on to your hats, boys and girls. These assorted millionaires have to make the ultimate sacrifice. They have to promise to pay for their own vacations, their own rounds of golf, and even — dare I say it? — their own lunches!

Now, please understand, I am not claiming to be a saint. Heck, if I were in congress on Pork Barrel Day and a lobbyist offered me $10 million to vote for some unnecessary bridge being built in Alaska or for a highway leading from no place to nowhere in West Virginia, I just might take it.

But, for crying out loud, how proud can I be when people boast about America's having the best politicians money can buy when I know the bozos can be had for the price of a coat, a stereo, or even a ham sandwich?!

· 27 ·
The Not So Noble Prize

There is probably nothing that people would rather have mentioned in their obituaries than the fact that along the way they had won a Nobel Prize. And it's not just the money, either, although 1.3 million smackers is nothing to sneeze at. No, what makes the Nobel Prize so prized is the prestige it gives the recipients. If you are lucky enough to win one, you will forever be known as Nobel Prize winner Burt Prelutsky or whatever your own name happens to be, and your words, even those on subjects far removed from the field for which you were honored, will be taken terribly seriously by a very gullible public.

I mean, you only have to look at some of the folks who have taken home the prize to recognize its hallowed place in the world. The list includes the likes of Ivan Pavlov, Sir Alexander Fleming, Marie and Pierre Curie, Harold Urey, Niels Bohr, Enrico Fermi, Francis Crick, James Watson, and Albert Einstein. Personally, I have no problem with such honorees. I mean, even though what I know about chemistry, medicine, physiology, and physics could be inscribed on the head of a small pin, I am willing to accept that their contributions were remarkable. And if dynamite inventor Alfred Nobel had left it at that, I'd have no problem with the Prize; I mean, aside from my never having won it. Of course I'm aware that even in the sciences people grovel for glory and will happily stab a colleague in the back if it improves their chances for Nobel recognition. But at least these folks are responsible for actual achievements.

They discovered things like penicillin, radium, heavy hydrogen, and the double helix.

I suppose because they had all this extra dynamite money lying around, the Scandinavians felt the need to invent a new category called economic sciences. Suddenly every two-bit economist woke up to discover that no matter how loony an economic scheme he came up with, he stood a good chance of winning a cool million in the Swedish lottery. In fact, one woman, in her divorce settlement from a professor of economics, insisted that she get half the loot if he copped a Prize within the following ten years. Sure enough, nine years and a few months later, the woman was $500,000 richer! I don't remember the guy's name, but it's a pretty safe guess that he was on the faculty at the University of Chicago. Nine of its professors have won the Prize in the past 40 years! By this time, they can pretty much promise new recruits a parking space, a discount in the faculty lounge, and a Nobel Prize of their very own.

But my real beef with the Nobel enterprise is with two other categories — literature and peace. And, no, I'm not bitter that in spite of my sterling prose, I haven't been invited to don tails and give a stirring, but humorous, acceptance speech in Stockholm. For one thing, I don't own a pair of tails, and, for another, I hate flying. And while I have no argument with such honorees as Rudyard Kipling, George Bernard Shaw, and John Steinbeck, and I am even willing to grant that writers such as William Faulkner, Eugene O'Neill, and Jean-Paul Sartre just might be acquired tastes that I never acquired, how did they come up with Giosue Carducci, Yasunari Kawabata, and Shmuel Agnon?

I'm not suggesting that Carducci, Kawabata, and Agnon aren't worthy of literary laurels. How could I? I've never even heard of them. What I do know is that they wrote in Italian, Japanese, and Hebrew, respectively. Are you going to tell me that anyone at the Swedish Academy read them in their original language? Baloney! It's my hunch that periodically the Swedes simply decide it's Japan's turn to win, or Italy's, or Israel's.

What makes me even more convinced this is the case is the hooey they concoct as a reason for lavishing fame and fortune on the poor sap. About Carducci, they rhapsodized: "A tribute to the creative energy, freshness of style, and lyrical force which characterize his poetic masterpieces." About Kawabata: "For his narrative mastery, which with great sensibility expresses the essence of the Japanese mind." And in praise of Agnon: "For his profoundly characteristic narrative art with motifs from the life of the Jewish people."

And then there's poor Wole Soyinka, the pride and joy of Nigeria, who had to stand there in his best bib and tucker and keep a straight face while some Swedish gentleman actually said, "Mr. Soyinka, who in a wide cultural perspective and with poetic overtones, fashions the drama of existence."

I suppose the fellow who writes this stuff will someday win a Nobel Prize of his own "for churning out high-sounding bilge year in and year out, expressing the Scandinavian fondness for unfathomable twaddle."

For good measure, between 1901 and 1910, which was when Sam Clemens died, they managed to give the prize to the likes of Sully Prudhomme, Christian Mommsen, Bjorstjerne Bjornson, Frederic Mistral, Jose Echegaray y Eizaguirre, Henryk Sienkiewicz, Rudolf Eucken, Selma Lagerlof, and Paul Heyse, but not to the author of *The Adventures of Huckleberry Finn* and *Tom Sawyer.* I wonder if Sully or Jose or Bjorstjerne thought, when they received the good news, that they might have gotten Mark Twain's mail by mistake.

But even the obvious shortcomings of the literature award can't compare to the absurdity of the peace prize. It isn't simply that the award has gone home with such villains as Le Duc Tho, Kofi Annan, and Yasser Arafat. It has also left Sweden in Jimmy Carter's suitcase, and in the luggage of scores of other self-righteous, lame-brained pacifists over the past 104 years.

This isn't to suggest that people like George Marshall, Elie Wiesel, and the Dalai Lama don't deserve our good thoughts, but I'd have thought better of them if they'd said thanks, but no thanks. I mean, the chairman of the peace committee, in honoring Carter, made it clear that they were using him as a means by which to vilify President Bush for invading Iraq. And there you have a clue to the reason I despise Carter and the Norwegian Nobel Committee — and please don't ask me why the Swedes outsourced the peace prize selection to Norway. I hate Carter because he was so hungry for the tawdry honor that he grasped it to his bosom even though he knew he was only getting it because the presenters needed a stalking horse in order to insult his president and his country.

But, Carter aside, I hate the peace prize because it never goes to anyone who is waging war. These knuckleheads refuse to acknowledge that sometimes peace can only be achieved by those willing to confront and defeat evil. Peace, after all, is easy enough to achieve. All you need is to never oppose tyranny. So it is that no awards were presented between 1914 and 1919, except in 1917, when it went to the International Committee of the Red Cross. Then again, no peace awards between 1939 and 1943. Then, in 1944 — surprise, surprise — the International Committee of the Red Cross won again.

Inasmuch as they often honor groups and not merely individuals, wouldn't you think the Scandinavians would have acknowledged their own debt to the R.A.F. and the British civilians who risked their lives to rescue the soldiers at Dunkirk? After all, the Nazis were well on their way to weaning the Swedes and the Norwegians off meatballs and on to bratwurst.

Why didn't they give it to FDR or, better yet, Winston Churchill? No, Sir Winston didn't win a Nobel Prize for helping to defeat Nazi

Germany. He finally got it in 1953 — for literature, for crying out loud! — "for his mastery of historical and biographical description as well as for brilliant oratory in defending exalted human values."

I can't help thinking that Sir Winston would have preferred winning it "for having tied a tin can to der fuhrer's fanny."

• 28 •
Dollars and Sense

Unlike everybody else in this country, I do not consider myself an expert when it comes to economics. I never took a course. I don't read *The Wall Street Journal.* I never even had an opinion about Alan Greenspan.

Still and all, that doesn't prevent me from having two really solid ideas. The first is that we eliminate the IRS. The second is that we eliminate the minimum wage.

Taking first things first, there is a reason that Robin Hood is a heroic figure. It wasn't simply that he stole from the rich and gave to the poor. Hell, the Democrats do that all the time, and no one would ever confuse Ted Kennedy or Hillary Clinton with a hero. No, what put Robin Hood right up there in the ranks of King Arthur, Prince Valiant, and Ivanhoe is the fact that he waged war against the tax collector.

I, myself, had intimate dealings with the IRS during the 1990s. The media assured us that, thanks to some negative publicity about their nasty tactics, the agency had turned over a new, gentler and kinder, leaf. Clearly, the media bought into the press releases. I, on the other hand, can assure you that America's tax collectors never lost their ability to give leeches lessons in blood-sucking.

Because I had had a bad turn in my writing career, my wife and I had to file for bankruptcy. The one creditor, we discovered, that's exempt from such matters is — you guessed it! — Internal Revenue. When you owe money to that outfit, the interest they charge gives new meaning to usury. It's enough to make Tony Soprano drool into his pasta fazul.

Unlike the Mafia, though, the IRS doesn't have to employ goons to collect. Because they automatically place a lien on your property, all they have to do if you miss a payment is back the truck up to your front door and cart off all your worldly goods.

The biggest difference between the Cosa Nostra and Internal Revenue is that the Italians dress better.

Which brings us to my second financial brainstorm. Every few years, the ladies and gentlemen in Congress go trolling for votes by deciding to increase the minimum wage. Each time they do it, we hear the same self-serving rhetoric from most Democrats and far too many Republicans. They bring out the crying towels as they sniffle over the plight of men — usually illegal aliens — trying to support their families on a miserable four or five or six dollars an hour.

When you hear these tales of financial woe, you have to be a pretty cold-hearted bastard not to be moved to tears. No matter how you start out thinking about the issue, when you begin picturing some poor kids going cold and hungry, that dollar-an-hour pay hike doesn't seem like such a big deal.

And that's when the liberals, like Martians in the movies, whisk you up in their spaceship, where their mad scientists complete the job of transforming your brains to mush. Where did you think all the pod people, otherwise known as left-wingers, came from anyway?

Somewhere along the way, you see, the Democrats turned the minimum wage on its head. Suddenly, menial jobs that used to go to high school kids saving up for a Saturday night movie were supposed to enable unskilled adults to support a wife and kids.

I may never win the Nobel Prize for economics, but even I know the difference between a living wage and a dating wage.

• 29 •

Mass Hysteria Is Hysterical

When I was a mere sprout, I recall that some nincompoops were convinced that fluoridating water was a Communist plot. So it was at a very tender age that I first caught on that, no matter how normal people might appear to be, there was always a good chance that scratch the surface and you'd find screwballs.

Nothing that I've experienced in all the ensuing years has done anything to dispel that belief. For instance, on occasion, when driving home late at night, I used to catch a bit of a radio call-in show hosted by a fellow named Art Bell. So far as I could tell, he devoted several hours every weeknight to discussing UFOs and extraterrestrials with his listeners. Now, I, personally, wouldn't want to devote 15 or 20 hours a week to discussing a really fascinating topic, such as baseball or myself. How Mr. Bell could bear to spend all those hours sharing gossip about Roswell, New Mexico, is totally beyond me. I only prayed that I'd never recognize one of those voices as belonging to a friend or neighbor.

These days, in order to remind myself that far too many of you have had your brains somehow replaced with pumpkin seeds, I tune in my friend Michael Medved's radio show on Wednesday. During the last of his three hours, he invites his audience to share their favorite conspiracy theories. The stuff and nonsense that many of you actually believe would be funny if it weren't so scary. I mean, some of you drive cars and work around heavy machinery and cast votes in national elections.

There is absolutely nothing so totally absurd, I'm convinced, that a fair number of our fellow Americans won't accept it as gospel. Which certainly explains cults, the *National Enquirer,* and Ted Kennedy's career.

It would be comforting to assume that these people are all illiterate bumpkins who think the earth is flat and the moon is made of gorgonzola. But, judging by the way they sound on the radio, that's not the case. It isn't the way they speak, but what they say, that's the tip-off to the fact that, mentally speaking, they're ninety-three cents shy of a dollar, three quarters shy of a football game, several sausage links shy of a Denny's Grand Slam.

But in spite of all that, these dimwits are in excellent company. Consider America's scientific community. Does a single day pass that the folks in the lab coats don't warn us that something or other is going to kill us before next Tuesday? They're the sort who give hysterics a bad name.

It would be a lot easier to take global warming seriously if 30 years ago, the same gang hadn't been warning us that global cooling was going to turn us all into Popsicles!

Now, I like a good scare as well as the next guy, but I'm far likelier to get goose bumps at the thought of a giant meteor heading our way, or even at the mere rumor of an Adam Sandler movie marathon, than at the prospect of polar ice caps melting. How frightened can I get at the thought that over the next few hundred or thousand years, the ocean level will rise five or six inches — especially when global cooling is just as likely to reverse the process?

By the way, wasn't acid rain supposed to defoliate the entire eastern seaboard long before now? And wasn't our food supply supposed to become exhausted once the world's population hit five billion? And weren't we all supposed to be going to war, not over oil, but over water by this time?

Frankly, I can't imagine how Tipper Gore manages to put up with that nervous Nellie she's married to. I always picture Al leaping up on a chair at the sight of a mouse and screaming, "Bubonic plague!"

All I can say is, it's a crying shame that Chicken Little is no longer among us. The sad truth is that if Professor Little were alive today, he could get a multi-million dollar grant to study the imminent falling of the sky.

• 30 •
The Star-Mangled Banner

There's probably no single piece of writing in this country that's as controversial or as likely to lead to fistfights as the U.S. Constitution. It's difficult to decide which portion of the document gets people riled up the most. At times, it almost seems to change on a daily basis. On Monday, it could be gun ownership, with folks like Michael Moore frothing at the mouth at the mere thought that a law-abiding citizen might own a weapon. You'd think Moore was planning to burgle your home the way he frets over the possibility you might actually be armed.

On Tuesday, it could be the pointy-headed crowd at the ACLU that's in full throttle, demanding that illegal aliens are entitled to all the rights and privileges of American citizens, not to mention a chicken in every pot.

But, as a rule, if you're really in the mood to see blood spilled, take advantage of your right to free speech by taking a position on the First Amendment. For instance, there are those who argue there should be absolutely no limits on free speech, even when it comes to pornography, blasphemy, or sedition. For all I know, they might even object to libel and slander laws, seeing them as infringements on the people's inalienable right to lie their heads off. These same zealots would probably object to the injunction against screaming "Fire!" in a crowded theater. To me, such an interpretation of the amendment is not only insane, but insulting to the fellows who hammered out the Constitution two centuries ago in Philadelphia.

Whatever else Franklin, Madison, and the rest of the boys may have been, they were not lunatics.

Lately, I've been hearing news that Congress may pass a law making the burning of the flag illegal. Emotionally, as the son of Russian immigrants who came to this country in the hope of finding a better life, and discovered that reality for once exceeded even their wildest dreams, I can well understand the motivation. But I'm not sure I'd want to deny an American the right to burn a flag, so long as it's not the one in front of my house, as I think his puny act of adolescent rebellion merely lets the rest of us know what a pitiful buffoon and pathetic ingrate he is.

Not being a constitutional scholar, I am naturally reluctant to become too embroiled in these matters. However, there is one thing about which I have a strong opinion, and I find it odd that nobody else seems as incensed as I. I'm referring to the singing of our national anthem at public events.

Admittedly, "The Star-Spangled Banner" lacks a certain something, musically speaking. But over the years, singers ranging from my aunt Sara to Richard Tucker have been able to do it justice, merely by singing it simply and sincerely. But at some point during the past ten years or so, certain female singers have decided that the only way to perform it was as if they were auditioning to provide orgasms for a porno soundtrack.

Maybe I'm being too harsh. Perhaps these songbirds don't intend any disrespect to the anthem. Perhaps they simply don't understand that patriotism means loving your country, not having sex with it.

• 31 •

Dissecting Frogs

President Bush has my total sympathy. Aside from having to spend all his vacations in Crawford, the thing I would hate the most about his job would be having to deal with France. The French aren't all terrible. I have to keep reminding myself. After all, Voltaire, Toulouse-Lautrec, and Claude Debussy were French. *The Hunchback of Notre Dame* and *Les Miserables* were written by a Frenchman. A Frenchman designed and built the Statue of Liberty. Louis Pasteur was French, and so was Hilaire Degas. The truth, however, is that they all lived a very long time ago. The closer one comes to recent times, the harder it is to find a good one.

What makes the French so appalling isn't that they haven't turned out a Victor Hugo in a couple of hundred years. Who has? What makes them so insufferable is their constant air of superiority. They keep posturing as if they wrote the book on ethics, values, and culture when all they've really been churning out are cream sauces, red wine, and over-priced frocks.

Much has been made of the French fondness for Jerry Lewis movies. What they love about them is that they think his loud, brash, dull-witted simpletons are realistic portrayals of the typical American. We in America like to think guys like Jimmy Stewart and Clark Gable are us, but the French know better. But, then, they always do.

Sometimes, I think the French were put on earth for no other reason than to give Germany an over-inflated sense of their military prowess. Other times, I can't come up with any reason at all.

France's idea of military leaders have been Napoleon, who, like Hitler, couldn't defeat the Russians or the English; the anti-Semitic generals who framed Capt. Dreyfus for treason; Marshal Henri Petain, who collaborated with the Nazis; and Gen. Charles de Gaulle, whose army was routed by the Huns in about a week. It's odd the way people always make fun of the Italian army and pretend the French are born warriors. In a war between the two, the Italians would clobber them in a day and a half — and then write a very nice opera about it.

Culturally speaking, France's major contributions during the past century were a couple of asterisks named Albert Camus and Jean-Paul Sartre. They promoted a French item called Existentialism. It was less a philosophy than a fad. Think of it as EST with a side order of escargots. Its main tenet was that life is pointless. Actually, it was Existentialism that was pointless. But it provided French guys, who wore black turtlenecks and smoked cheap cigarettes in Parisian cafes, with world-weary pickup lines to use on girls from Kansas.

Existentialism was the philosophical equivalent of auteurism — that silly critical con game propagated by Cahiers du Cinema. Its disciples would go so far as to insist, for instance, that *The Crimson Kimono* and *The Magnificent Matador* were better movies than *It's a Wonderful Life* and *On the Waterfront* because Sam Fuller and Budd Boetticher were *auteurs* while Frank Capra and Elia Kazan were merely directors.

During a heat wave a while back, over 12,000 elderly people died in France. What does that tell us? For one thing, it confirms that France is a Third-World nation. How else to explain their lack of air conditioning in the 21st century? Believe me, a country that likes to smoke, but not to bathe, is not a country that should turn its collective back on air conditioning.

What else does the death of those 12,000 old people tell us?

Well, obviously — and as usual — it tells us that the French cannot take the heat.

As for their own reaction to the enormous tragedy, it seems that the Frogs, a notoriously unsentimental people, have chosen to look upon it as merely the thinning of *le herd.*

• 32 •
A Plea to Unendow the Arts

For years, I have argued against the very existence of the National Endowment of the Arts. If an artist can't be self-sustaining in a capitalist country as large and as rich as America, he should get into another line of work. It's certainly not the business of the politicians and the bureaucrats, who you notice aren't spending their own money, to support him and his artistic pipedreams.

If 300 million of us have decided we don't wish to underwrite inferior work, where do a handful of senators and congressmen get off wasting millions of our tax dollars to keep these dilettantes in beer and Skittles?

Understand, I'm a live-and-let-live kind of guy, and I have no problem with the private sector squandering its own money any way it likes. Heck, if the trustees of the MacArthur Foundation see fit to bestow $300,000 grants on a bunch of weirdos who write Eskimo poetry or build sand castles, that's their affair. Still, I can't imagine why they'd rather give all that money to some beatnik who makes giraffes out of pipe cleaners, and will probably blow the dough on cheap hooch and wild women, when they could just as easily give it to me, knowing that I will use it to buy tax-free munis.

Almost every time you read about a community going berserk over an art exhibit that is either sheer pornography or re-creates the Christmas crèche using animal blood and human excrement, you can rest assured it's your tax dollars at work.

Recently, I read about a controversial artwork that, for once, wasn't underwritten by the feds. This time, I'm pleased to report, it was only the good citizens of Livermore, California, who got taken to the cleaners.

It seems the city fathers had $40,000 lying around, so they decided to commission a ceramic mural to grace the exterior of the new library. For some reason, they decided that the perfect artist was someone named Maria Alquilar. I'm not certain why, of all the artists in America who would kill for a $40,000 payday, she was selected. Only a cynical old poop would hazard a guess that her selection may have had more to do with Ms. Alquilar's race and gender than with her natural talent. Whatever the reason, it obviously had nothing to do with her spelling ability.

For when the 16-foot-wide work was unveiled, 11 of the 175 famous names had been misspelled! They included the likes of Einstein, Shakespeare, Van Gogh, and Michelangelo. On the bright side, Ms. Alquilar got 164 of them right.

In her own defense, the lady said, "The importance of this work is that it is supposed to unite people….The mistakes wouldn't even register with a true artisan. The people that are into humanities, they are not looking at the words. In their mind, the words register correctly."

The city council, clearly not into the humanities, subsequently voted to pay the artist an additional $6,000, plus expenses, to fly cross country from her new studio in Miami to correct her spelling errors.

Now do you see why it's such a stupid idea to allow public servants to dabble in the arts? A private citizen would know better than to fork over the entire $40,000 before the job was finished. You or I certainly wouldn't pay even more money so that Ms. Alquilar can repair the damage. She'd do it or we'd sue her ass in small-claims court! But, then, you and I don't go around commissioning art; we know there's already plenty of the stuff lying around, and without spelling mistakes.

Hell, I'd sue Alquilar just for being so damn snotty, and trying to turn illiteracy into a virtue.

I suppose, to be fair about it, she did get most of the names right. So one could look at the big picture — or ceramic mural, as it were — and ask whether the glass is half full or half empty.

Speaking of that particular glass, I have long wondered who came up with that line, which so neatly defines the distinction between pessimism and optimism. I suspect it might have been the very same fellow who first moved the couch out of the living room and into the office, Sigmund Freud. Or, as Ms. Alquilar might put it — and very likely did on the Livermore mural — Cigmond Fried.

· 33 ·

In Praise of Oil

Please pay close attention because we're going to be discussing numbers, and I happen to know that most of you are lousy at math.

In 1933, a movie ticket cost a quarter, a hamburger was a dime, and a soda pop was a nickel. Assuming you actually had a dollar in 1933, you could go out on a date for a dollar and come home with change.

In 1936, a gallon of gas cost 25 cents. A year later, my dad bought a new Plymouth sedan for less than $800. In 1946, it was the car he was still driving when our family moved from Chicago to L.A.

In 1949, a 14-oz bottle of ketchup cost 15 cents, and a T-bone steak cost 55 cents a pound.

My reason for giving you this brief history in practical economics is to point out that the price of gas has only gone up about 10-fold in 68 years. Compare it to some of those other everyday items. Do you think you could buy a new automobile for $7,800? Buy any T-bones lately for $5.50? Get into any first-run movies for $2.50? You can't even buy a bag of popcorn for that price. And try spending 40 cents on your first date, and I can guarantee you won't have a second.

So, why is it that it's only the price of gasoline that makes so many people go berserk? I believe it's because the Left has politicized petroleum. We've all heard them ranting: "No blood for oil." They insist that George Bush took America to war because of it. They ignore the fact that the Iraqis now own their own oil, and they ignore, too, the indisputable fact that Bush is clearly pro-Israel, although Israel's only oil source is olives.

I'll admit that I can imagine going to war over oil, just as I can well imagine going to war over water. Oil, after all, is as essential to an industrialized nation as water is to the survival of an individual.

It would be nice if we could free ourselves of our dependence on Arab nations and Russia for our energy, but sun power and wind power just won't cut it. Ironically, the same tree-huggers who resent this dependence also oppose mining for coal, drilling for Alaskan oil, and using nuclear energy. These are the same Neanderthals who rail that Republican Bush doesn't make a move without first checking with the Saudis, even though the Saudis urged him not to take out Saddam Hussein, but never get around to explaining why Kennedy, Johnson, Carter, and Clinton did nothing to free us of the necessity to go hat-in-hand to the Arabs.

Frankly, I find it amazing that in spite of wars, inflation and greed, gas has only increased by a thousand percent in about 70 years, and, moreover, has been greatly improved during that time. Wouldn't you think there'd be a bigger stink raised about the price of movies having gone up three thousand percent, while having only gotten worse during that same period?

So, my question is this: Where in the Bill of Rights is it written that filling up your SUV should cost you the same as it cost your grandpa to gas up his Model-T?

In conclusion, let me just say that anybody in the ponytail-and-granny-glasses crowd who sincerely believes that oil isn't all that important is free to do without, thus creating a surplus and thereby lowering the cost for those of us who actually live in the 21st century.

Chapter Six

INDIA HAS ITS SACRED COWS
WE HAVE OUR SACRED BULLS

• 34 •
The Wedding Wars

Thanks to a lot of gay people who don't know when they have it good, there is a controversy raging in America over who has the right to get married. At times, it must appear to the young women of this nation that the only men who are eager to tie the knot are homosexuals.

I happen to be of two minds on the issue. On the one hand, I am a traditionalist. I believe in marriage between a man and a woman. Yet, honesty dictates that I confess to having been thrice-married. So, in my case at least, it's been a man and three women.

A strong argument in favor of gay unions is that it would benefit the economy. More marriages means more engagement rings, wedding gifts, bachelor dinners, floral bouquets, and, inevitably, more work for divorce attorneys.

As someone with strong libertarian leanings, I don't really care what anybody does so long as it doesn't infringe on my freedoms or my satellite reception. So if two men decide they want to pledge their troth, I figure it's none of my business, so long as I don't have to dance with the bride.

The only problem I really foresee is that once you open the door to state-sanctioned unions between two consenting adults, on what basis do you ban marriages between brother and sister, or brother and brother? What logical argument can you then make against joining father and daughter, or mother and son? Or Pamela Sue Anderson and the Oakland Raiders?

Is anybody seriously going to argue that the integrity of the gene pool mustn't be tainted by such unnatural couplings? All you have to do is tune in the Jerry Springer show to realize that it's way too late to slam that particular barn door.

Some people would argue that same-sex marriages should be illegal because the singular purpose of marriage is the creation of children. If that were the case, you would next have to outlaw unions between people in their sixties and seventies, and between younger couples who have no wish to propagate the species.

As you see, it is next to impossible to define exactly what constitutes or should constitute a marriage. To those on either side who insist that the sole determining factor should be the desire to commit to a lifelong union, I can only say, "Hold on! Not so darn fast!" God knows I hate to be a wet blanket. But I'm not so sure I'm all that anxious for the state of California to give its official blessing to that very special loving relationship that exists between my dog Duke and my right leg!

• 35 •
Anchors Aweigh

Ever since I can remember, we've treated TV news anchors as if they were a combination of royalty and high priests. Any time one of them dies or even retires, we carry on as if the flags should be lowered to half-mast. It's ridiculous, and, worse yet, it's unseemly.

Please understand, I'm not taking this opportunity to jump on Dan Rather. After all, he, at least, is leaving under a cloud, his reputation in tatters — and not just because he's spent the past several years running third in a three-dog ratings race with Brokaw and Jennings.

You can go back to Chet Huntley, David Brinkley, John Chancellor, and Walter Cronkite. We treated them all with a deference that was totally out of proportion to the work they did. Essentially, the job description requires that they read the captions to the news footage we're watching and to introduce the on-site reporters. Do you really think that constitutes the mental equivalent of heavy lifting? For doing what your Uncle Sid could do — and with a lot more pizzazz — they're paid enormous amounts of money. On top of all the dough, they are constantly the honorees at testimonial dinners, but that's fine, so long as I don't have to attend. But the trouble is, they're regarded as important people by way too many of us, and that's not good. Why? Because it makes us all look like a bunch of saps — what H.L. Mencken called the *boobus americanus* and what P.T. Barnum simply labeled suckers.

Because these anchors get to spend their entire careers talking about important events and important people, they naturally come to regard themselves as important. Self-delusion is a form of insanity and we should not encourage it by fawning over them.

When they finally sign off for the last time, you notice that the testimonials inevitably mention how many political conventions they covered, how many space missions, how many inaugurations, assassinations, uprisings, and wars, as if they had had a hand in any of these earth-shaking events. It wasn't their hands that were involved, it was their behinds, as they sat year after year at those desks, declaiming in those store-bought voices what we were seeing with our own eyes — all thanks to the journalistic peons who actually went places and did things and took risks so that we could sit home and watch it. Now, I'm not saying we should kill the messengers. I'm just suggesting it's time we stopped canonizing them.

• 36 •

Pride Goeth Before a Parade

Recently, the media has been all atwitter over gay-related matters. What with the move to legalize gay marriages, the Supreme Court's giving sodomy its version of the Good Housekeeping Seal of Approval, loveable gays in movies and all over TV, and a virtual gaggle of gay pride parades, you could easily get the impression that America has gone gaga over gayhood.

Unlike most people who claim they don't care what consenting adults do in the privacy of their bedroom, I really mean it. When you get right down to it, nearly everything that other people do, from playing golf to guzzling beer, strikes me as irrational. But I have to acknowledge that it's really none of my business. I don't even care if people use drugs. Where do I get off telling others not to shoot heroin or snort cocaine if that's what the geeks enjoy?

My only concern is with antisocial behavior that injures other people. So, I'd turn a blind eye to all the empty whisky bottles in my neighbor's trash barrel so long as he didn't beat his kids or run down a pedestrian as a result of his drinking. However, if he crossed that line, I'd throw the book at him. And he wouldn't get to cop a plea on the grounds that he was a victim, himself — a victim of bad old John Barleycorn. I hold everyone responsible for his own actions. I blame the shooter, not the gun. It seems pretty clear that God believes in self-will. And so do I.

My only problem with gay men is that their lifestyle very often leads to AIDS, and that single disease is draining off far too much research funding from diseases that aren't the direct result of promiscuous sexual behavior.

Until medical science comes up with cures for, say, leukemia, Parkinson's, and Alzheimers, I'll resent every nickel that's deflected to finding a cure for AIDS. To hear the well-orchestrated wails from the gay community, you'd think the government was short-changing research in that area because of homophobia. The fact is, the gays, thanks to their political clout and their disproportionately huge numbers in high-profile Hollywood, have strong-armed hundreds of millions of dollars for their own cause. Every time you spotted one of those ubiquitous red ribbons or saw Elizabeth Taylor at some gala fundraiser, you should have been thinking of some little kid dying of cancer instead of Ed Harris in *The Hours*.

Frankly, I'd like to know how grown men, who are famous for regarding themselves as sensitive and compassionate — the same men who insist on having unprotected anal intercourse and wind up afflicted with AIDS — feel they're entitled to research funds that might otherwise go to save suffering children.

Understand, I truly have no problem with homosexuals being homosexual. I wouldn't go so far as to say that some of my best friends are gay, but, having worked in show business for thirty-five years, I've known a lot of them and I've liked a lot of them. In fact, I've never figured out why so many heterosexual men seem to despise gays. All I can say is that when I was younger and actively engaged in the pursuit of women, I appreciated every bright, successful, good-looking man who wasn't a competitor.

I know that some people hypothesize that inside every macho gay-basher is an interior decorator screaming to get out and do something about those drapes in the living room. Maybe, but I doubt it. By that reasoning, every anti-Semite is really dying to study Torah and start observing the Sabbath a day early.

What does confound me about gays is their constant need to

parade. What's that all about? I realize that, for some of them, there is a deep-seated desire to play dress-up. More power to them. But from whence springs this insatiable need to create gridlock?

And what the hell is gay pride all about? Coming out of the closet is one thing, but coming all the way out into the middle of the street and disrupting city traffic is just plain rude.

Finally, why on earth should anybody be so darn proud to be gay? I'm not saying they should be ashamed of who they are. But from everything I've read and heard, people are simply born that way. It's all in the chromosomes, they insist. Fine. I accept that they're born gay, just as others are born heterosexual. But if that's the case, what cause have they to be proud of it? If it's not an acquired talent, a learned skill, not even a minor accomplishment, then it's tantamount to being proud to have red hair or green eyes or, you should pardon the expression, a straight nose. However, that's not pride, it's vanity.

When you get right down to it, Bach, Shakespeare, and Pasteur, to name just a few high-achievers, never felt the need to march in some silly parade in downtown San Francisco. So, how is it that every other day, or so it seems, a thousand guys whose only claim to fame is based on the particular orifice into which they prefer to insert their male organ can't resist the urge to merge on Market Street?

Chapter Seven

UNFORTUNATELY, LONG AFTER
MOSES PARTED THE RED SEA,
THERE REMAINS A SEA
OF JEWISH REDS

· 37 ·
Some of My Best Friends
Used to Be Jews

Several years ago, when I was reviewing movies for the UCLA *Daily Bruin,* I got in hot water for panning *Pepe* and *Exodus* in the same issue. The *Bruin* editor and the head of publications for the university got called on the carpet by the president of the Directors Guild of America, George Sidney. He threatened to cut off grants and scholarships to the theater arts department unless I was canned. Like most Hollywood types, he was a true zealot when it came to free speech…except when he wasn't.

At the meeting, to which I was not invited, Sidney, who had produced and directed *Pepe,* an expensive bomb starring Cantinflas, claimed he didn't care what I wrote about his own movie, but that anybody who would dare give *Exodus* a bad review had to be an anti-Semite. When the editor told him that I was Jewish, Mr. Sidney, I was told, slammed his fist on the desk and announced, "They're the worst kind!"

At the time, I thought it was one of the funniest things I had ever heard. This is to report that I have finally stopped laughing.

When I find American Jews in the forefront when it comes to denouncing President Bush while dismissing Saddam Hussein as just another minor nuisance; when I find American Jews leading the parade of appeasers; when I find Jews sympathizing with the plight of Islamo fascists and labeling homicide bombers as freedom fighters willing to die for their beliefs; I find myself thinking that George Sidney was right on the money.

Many, way too many, of my fellow Jews are those most vocal on insisting that only the U.N. has the moral authority to determine America's foreign policy. This is the same world body that elected Libya to head up its commission on human rights. In terms of logic, this is akin to hiring Wile E.Coyote to guard your chicken coop. In terms of morality, it is something far worse.

In what bizarro universe would you commit to a policy only when and if it were first approved by China, France, and Russia — three nations you wouldn't trust to tell you the time of day?

Most of the canards regarding President Bush are eagerly promoted by American Jews in and out of the media. It is most often they who insist, for instance, that his only reason for attacking Iraq is his desire to gain control of Saddam Hussein's oil fields. While it's true that the entire world should devoutly wish to see Iraq's oil profits being spent for something other than palaces and munitions, what gives anybody the idea that we would ever confiscate Iraqi property? Has anyone noticed the American flag waving over Kuwait City?

It's particularly reprehensible for American Jews to treat Bush to the constant tirade of lies and insults. After all, even the Arabs complain about his close ties to Israel — the one nation in the area, we should all keep in mind, without oil reserves!

Speaking of Israel, why is it that American Jews and journalists so often insist on using the term "occupied territories"? During World War II, Germany occupied Poland, Holland, France, Norway, etc. Japan occupied China, Mongolia, the Philippines, etc. For years, the Soviet Union occupied Hungary, East Germany, Poland, Czechoslovakia, etc. We all understood that when a sovereign nation was invaded and conquered by another country, it was occupied. The fact that Israel has offered, in hopes of achieving a lasting peace, to cede land to its enemies has been turned on its head. The Arab refugees never had a nation; the so-called "occupied territories" were formerly parts of Jordan and Egypt. When those countries decided to join others in attacking Israel, they wound up losing some of their turf. That's the way it often works when you start a war and lose.

The real question remains, why do so many American Jews insist on identifying with people who share none of their democratic ideals, who parade their dead through the streets, lionize the killers of babies and old people, treat women as chattel, and would gladly turn the clock back to the ninth century? There is no rational reason why in a society that is increasingly secular, my fellow Jews have made something of a religion out of casting stones at Bush, Israel, and the Republican party.

It took me four decades, but I finally comprehend how correct George Sidney was when he made his pronouncement. But I still stick to my guns — *Exodus* was a real stinker.

· 38 ·

Jews and the Evangelicals

It is a peculiar thing about Jews that we seem to trust our enemies more than we do our friends. Maybe that's because, historically, we at least had the comfort of knowing where we stood with those who openly despised us, but we very often suffered betrayal from our alleged allies.

It would help explain why many of my older relatives, those who had been born in Czarist Russia and had experienced pogroms, believed in Stalin and eagerly lapped up his propaganda. Because he was an enemy of their enemies, they foolishly mistook him for a friend. It's simplistic, but why else would so many seemingly well-informed American Jews have enlisted in the Communist Party, swelling the ranks of Stalin's "useful idiots"?

These days, the most consistently pro-Israel group of Americans, oddly enough, is evangelical Christians. A sane and rational person might assume that fact would be appreciated and applauded by us. By and large, however, that isn't the case. Many of my fellow Jews don't like or trust devout Christians. When I ask them why, they suddenly become history professors. To listen to them, you'd think the Inquisition had ended earlier this year. Frankly, when I hear them dredging up ancient animosities, I'm surprised they haven't taken a page out of the Al Sharpton playbook and demanded reparations from Spain!

When I point out that Jews have enjoyed unprecedented freedom and prosperity in a Christian nation — namely, the United States —

my friends insist that it's not Christian. At which point, I have to laugh.

The fact that we're not a theocracy does not make their case, no matter how loudly they may insist on it. When we say that Turkey, for instance, is an Islamic nation and that India is Hindu and that Italy is Catholic, although none of them is a theocratic state, how can we deny that America, whose population is overwhelmingly Christian — and is only 2% Jewish — is Christian?! The fact of the matter is that America has a higher proportion of Christians than Israel has of Jews.

The problem between pro-Israel Jews and pro-Israel evangelicals is that the Christians believe that, come Judgment Day, Jews will have to convert to the true faith or be doomed for all eternity. Big deal. There are millions of people who believe that Elvis is alive, that James Dean will stage a comeback as soon as the scars heal, and even that the Cubs will go all the way this year!

I have no way of knowing if Christians are correct in believing that the Messiah is coming back a second time, or if Jews are right in thinking that Jesus was a first-rate prophet but not quite up to raising the dead. Where faith is concerned, I don't take sides.

In case you haven't guessed, I'm not religiously oriented. However, I'm for anything that helps people behave decently and helps them cope with all the inevitable tragedies of life, up to and including death. In my experience, anyway, most religions in America perform those functions more often than not.

Understand, I do not support Israel because it's a Jewish state. I am on its side because it is, one, a democracy in a part of the world where democracy is as alien as barbecued pork; two, it is a staunch ally of America; and, three, for over fifty years, although it has been besieged by terrorist states and fanatical killers, it has displayed remarkable restraint. It is a restraint that, I humbly confess, I could not duplicate in my wildest dreams.

So when I hear American Jews who, as often as not, are no more religious than I, dismiss Christian sympathizers, I say to them: "So you believe one thing about Jesus and they believe another. So what? Who cares? If it makes you happy, make a bet with an evangelical, and in a million years or whenever the great Hallelujah Day rolls around, one of you will owe the other one five bucks. In the meanwhile, in a world in which Israel's opponents outnumber her supporters by at least five hundred-to-one, it's high time you learned to distinguish between friend and foe."

• 39 •
The Jewish Grinch Who Stole Christmas

I never thought I'd live to see the day that Christmas would become a dirty word. You think it hasn't? Then why is it that people are being prevented from saying it in polite society for fear that it will offend?

Schools are being forced to replace "Christmas vacation" with "winter break" in their printed schedules. At Macy's, the word is verboten even though they've made untold millions of dollars from their sympathetic portrayal in the Christmas classic, *Miracle on 34th Street.* Carols, even instrumental versions, are banned in certain places. A major postal delivery service has not only made their drivers doff their Santa caps, but ordered them not to decorate their trucks with Christmas wreaths.

How is it, one well might ask, that in a Christian nation this is happening? And in case you find that designation objectionable, would you deny that India is a Hindu country, that Pakistan is Muslim, that Poland is Catholic? That doesn't mean those nations are theocracies. But when the overwhelming majority of a country's population is of one religion, and roughly 90% of Americans happen to be one sort of Christian or another, only a darn fool would deny the obvious.

Although it seems a long time ago, it really wasn't, that people who came here from other places made every attempt to fit in. Assimilation wasn't a threat to anyone; it was what the Statue of

Liberty represented. *E pluribus unum,* one out of many, was our motto. The world's melting pot was our nickname. It didn't mean that any group of people had to check their customs, culture, or cuisine at the door. It did mean that they, and especially their children, learned English, and that they learned to live and let live.

That has changed, you may have noticed. And I blame my fellow Jews. When it comes to pushing the multicultural, anti-Christian agenda, you find Jewish judges, Jewish journalists, and the ACLU at the forefront.

Being Jewish, I should report, Christmas was never celebrated by my family. But what was there not to like about the holiday? To begin with, it provided a welcome two week break from school. The decorated trees were nice, the lights were beautiful, *It's a Wonderful Life* was a great movie, and some of the best Christmas songs were even written by Jews.

But the dirty little secret in America is that anti-Semitism is no longer a problem in society; it's been replaced by a rampant anti-Christianity. For example, the hatred spewed towards George W. Bush has far less to do with his policies than it does with his religion. The Jews voice no concern when a Bill Clinton or a John Kerry makes a big production out of showing up at black Baptist churches or posing with Rev. Jesse Jackson because they understand that's just politics. They only object to politicians attending church for religious reasons.

My fellow Jews, who often have the survival of Israel heading the list of their concerns when it comes to electing a president, only gave 26% of their vote to Bush, even though he is clearly the most pro-Israel president we've ever had in the Oval Office.

It is the ACLU, which is overwhelmingly Jewish in terms of membership and funding, that is leading the attack against Christianity in America. It is they who have conned far too many people into believing that the phrase "separation of church and state" actually exists somewhere in the Constitution.

You may have noticed, though, that the ACLU is highly selective when it comes to religious intolerance. The same group of self-righteous shysters who, at the drop of a "Merry Christmas" will slap you with an injunction, will fight for the right of an American Indian to ingest peyote and a devout Islamic woman to be veiled on her driver's license.

I happen to despise bullies and bigots. I hate them when they represent the majority, but no less when, like Jews in America, they represent an infinitesimal minority.

I am getting the idea that too many Jews won't be happy until they pull off their own version of the Spanish Inquisition, forcing Christians to either deny their faith and convert to agnosticism or suffer the consequences.

I should point out that many of these people abhor Judaism every bit as much as they do Christianity. They're the ones who behave as if atheism were a calling. They're the nutcakes who go berserk if anyone even says, "In God we trust" or mentions that the Declaration of Independence refers to a Creator with a capital "C." By this time, I'm only surprised that they haven't begun a campaign to do away with Sunday as a day of rest. After all, it's only for religious reasons — Christian reasons — that Sunday, and not Tuesday or Wednesday, is so designated.

This is a Christian nation, my friends. And all of us are fortunate it is one, and that so many Americans have seen fit to live up to the highest precepts of their religion. Speaking as a member of a minority group — and one of the smaller ones at that — I say it behooves those of us who don't accept Jesus Christ as our savior to show some gratitude to those who do, and to start respecting the values and traditions of the overwhelming majority of our fellow citizens, just as we keep insisting that they respect ours.

Merry Christmas.

• 40 •
The Christmas Grinch Revisited

Nothing that I have ever written has provoked as huge a response as a piece I wrote recently called "The Jewish Grinch That Stole Christmas."

In the article, which brought me roughly ten times as much e-mail as I'm accustomed to, I suggested that my fellow Jews were at the forefront in waging war on the values and traditions of Christian Americans.

Predictably enough, the response from gentiles was uniformly positive. The feedback from Jews was somewhat less positive, roughly split between those who admired my courage and those who accused me of being a turncoat. What I found most telling was that those who damned me didn't, as a rule, refute what I had written; they were merely angry that a Jew had written the piece. They accused me of lending aid and comfort to bigots.

Because I make it a rule to write back to anyone who writes me, and because I assume that those who took the time and trouble to write were representative of many more who didn't, I'd like to share some of my responses.

The term that nearly every Jew used in condemning me was "a self-hating anti-Semite." A few accused me of not really being a Jew. That didn't mean they thought I was a Catholic or a Baptist flying under false colors; no, they meant that my sole claim to being Jewish was that my ancestors were Jewish. The fact is, they're right.

As I have written on other occasions, I am not a religious man. I do not keep kosher. I do not help make up the morning minyan at the local synagogue. I do not even attend High Holiday services. So what? I'm Jewish because I say I'm Jewish. And because, quite frankly, with my face, who would believe me if I bothered to deny it? Furthermore, most Jews in America are not orthodox and can not read Hebrew or even speak Yiddish. For the most part, American Jews are circumcised, have a bar mitzvah, attend a reformed or conservative temple twice a year, and vote the straight Democratic ticket.

Also, I say I'm Jewish because I don't wish to offend the memory of my parents by denying their religion and the religion of their parents.

Finally, I say I'm Jewish because Hitler would have said I was Jewish, and then sent me off to Auschwitz, if I hadn't been fortunate enough to have been born in America.

That was my whole point. I was lucky to have been born to a Jewish family in a Christian nation. It was, in the main, Christian soldiers who liberated the Nazi death camps. Even if I'm not as Jewish as some of my critics would like, I still believe it behooves us to be openly grateful to our Christian neighbors — not because we fear future pogroms — but because it's the decent thing to do.

One of the very few points for which I was specifically taken to task was for referring to America as a Christian nation. To those people, I pointed out that I wasn't claiming this nation is a theocracy, but Christians of one denomination or another compose about 90% of America's population. That is 10% higher than the percentage of Jews in Israel, but I am willing to wager that none of my critics would deny that Israel is a Jewish state.

The sad fact is that the ACLU is made up in good part of Jews, and it is that organization and its lawyers who are leading the assault against Christmas. What makes it particularly unfortunate is that most Jews are not only opposed to the policies of the ACLU, but are embarrassed by and ashamed of the organization. However, when every ACLU lawyer who appears on TV to announce the latest attempt to remove Christian symbols and traditions from America seems to be Jewish, it's all too easy for Christians to assume the rest of us support this vile campaign.

As one of my respondents put it, "An anti-Semite used to be someone who hated Jews, but it's become someone whom Jews hate." The problem with that truism is that Jews, in the great majority, don't hate gentiles. Sometimes it just seems that way. In fact, most of us are well aware that Israel has no more devoted allies in the world than America's most devout Christians.

Unfortunately, as is so often the case with black Americans, those who are high-profile and get most of the media attention are the radicals and the rabble-rousers.

When my critics accused me of promoting anti-Semitism, I pleaded not guilty. I asked them if they thought that gentiles were so stupid that, until I wrote my piece, they didn't recognize that there is a secular jihad underway in this country to remove Christ from Christmas.

Finally, the problem is that if Christians complain that the minority group is trying to bully the majority, they stand condemned as bigots. If I, a Jew, suggest that Christians should be free to celebrate one of their holier holidays in any fashion they like, and not have to feel guilty about it, I'm accused of being a self-hating anti-Semite. In short, nobody is allowed to be critical of Jews. Well, it so happens that while we Jews may be the Chosen People, that doesn't make us the perfect people. And, believe me, I'm not just talking about my relatives.

Many of us, Jews and Christians alike, have been annoyed with American Muslims because they seem to spend an inordinate amount of time whining about racial profiling at the airports, instead of condemning the worldwide butchery of Islamic fascists or passing the hat to place a reward on Osama bin Laden's head. Well, to me, the silence of American Jews when it comes to Christian-bashing has been equally deafening.

What truly astonishes me is the patience and good grace with which Christians have dealt with this attack on so many things they hold dear.

It is, I think, a tribute to their religion.

Chapter Eight

A FEW VERY GOOD MEN

• 41 •
The Anti-Military Militants

Last year, an acquaintance named Dave, a television writer who had fallen on hard times, decided to make an economy move to South Carolina. An indicator of his sour mood is that he now includes "The Swamp" in his e-mail address. I have every reason to believe that this Hollywood transplant isn't referring to the physical land-scape, but to the folks who live there. Over the past several months, he has made it perfectly clear that he feels as if he has awakened to find himself dwelling in Dogpatch.

As we all know, a certain amount of trauma takes place anytime we pack up. But that's especially the case when we set down 3,000 miles away. No longer do we know where the barbershop is or the dry cleaner or the coffee shop where they remember to drain the tuna before making your sandwich. If you add to the mix the fact that the man is middle-aged and thus regarded as over-the-hill in a business that confuses youth with ability, one can readily understand a certain amount of bitterness.

Even though I thought he was over-reacting to neighbors whom he felt were too devout in their religion and too conservative in their politics, I continued to feel he was more to be pitied than censured. But that all ended as of last week. In response to something I had written in favor of the war in Iraq, he took me and most of his fel-low Carolinians to task.

He e-mailed me a very curt note to let me know he was totally opposed to my position. He simply couldn't imagine how I could possibly be in favor of a war that had already seen five hundred American soldiers killed.

Of course, people opposed to the war — any war — always presume to have dibs on the moral high ground. Only they, they would insist, care about the youngsters who do the actual fighting. Only they are truly compassionate. Anything you say in opposition merely makes their case, proving that you are a bloodthirsty ogre who enjoys nothing better than the death and maiming of young Americans.

When you remind him, as I did, that he was one of those people who had prophesized that we would lose upwards of a hundred thousand troops during the invasion, he insists that the total number of casualties is inconsequential. So it's a waste of time pointing out what a tiny number of losses America has actually suffered in ending Hussein's evil regime, particularly when compared with the lives lost in single battles at places like Iwo Jima and Guadalcanal, Belleau Wood and the Battle of the Bulge.

So, instead, I argued that while I, too, hate the idea of young Americans dying, the fact remains that we have an all-volunteer military these days. One has to assume that when one voluntarily signs up to serve, one does so knowing the risk involved.

To which he replied, in that smug way that so many liberals adopt when being holier-than-thou: "Maybe because I live near Parris Island and see so many young Marines walking around, I believe I know better than you that these kids have no idea what they're letting themselves in for."

That did it. At that moment, my pity supply ran dry. It's one thing to disagree about George Bush's foreign policy. But to be that insufferably condescending about all the young men and women who have enlisted in the military is simply beyond the pale.

The scary thing is that I know any number of people who share his insufferable attitude.

Oddly enough, it is only when young people opt to devote some portion of their adult lives to serving their country that condescending liberals suddenly decide that they're too callow to make such important decisions. How is it if an 18-year-old decides to join the military, it's a sure sign of immaturity, but if he decides to become an insurance salesman, a stock broker or a priest, we're supposed to assume he's all grown up and knows what he's doing? Why do these people frown on the 18-year-olds who believe in defending America's freedom and liberty, but give a pat on the back to teenagers who go off to expensive universities in order to major in gay studies, pop culture or 19th-century Portuguese poetry?

One of the lame answers liberals will offer is that, in performing their military duty, the youngsters might get killed. Well, the fact of the matter is that not only does everybody die, but, war or no war, only the very elderly die at a faster clip than the young.

American teenagers commit suicide as if there's no tomorrow, thus ensuring that, for them, there won't be. Many more die as a result of drugs, either through using them or selling them on someone else's turf. Others die because they get drunk on a regular basis and end up driving their cars into telephone poles. So why is it that people such as Dave only seem to view their premature demises as tragic when they happen to die wearing a uniform?

What I find truly offensive about the liberals' point of view is that while they abhor the idea that their sons and daughters might even consider serving in the military, if their offspring decided to take up criminal law and spend the next fifty years springing serial killers and child molesters, these same parents would be popping their buttons and throwing a party.

I ended up by writing one final e-mail to Dave. I let him know I thought his attitude towards those Marines in his neighborhood was patronizing and presumptuous and that he had better keep his opinion to himself if he didn't want to get a well-deserved punch in the snoot. What's more, judging by the fact that in his mid-50s he felt he had no option but to move clear across the country to a place he obviously detested, he had a lot of chutzpah criticizing other people's career decisions.

• 42 •
A Hero's More Than a Sandwich

One of the good things that came out of the tragic events of 9/11 is that heroism has reacquired some of its original luster. I'm not certain when it lost it, not at all certain when bravery above and beyond the call of duty gave way to meaning nothing more or less than being in the wrong place at the wrong time.

Looking back, I have an idea it happened during the Jimmy Carter administration when hostages were taken in Tehran. People who had been abducted by the minions of Ayatollah Khomeini and held captive by Iranian thugs were being widely hailed as heroes by the American media.

I'm not suggesting that a hostage can't also be a hero. Apparently Sen. John McCain behaved as one when he was a POW, volunteering to be beaten by the Viet Cong in order to spare the men in his charge. But I'm afraid that your run-of-the-mill hostage is no more a hero than were any of the unfortunate passengers in the planes that were crashed into the World Trade Center.

It is appropriate to grieve for innocent victims, but we should stop short of lionizing them. Otherwise, how do we distinguish between those who simply die and those who perish trying to save others? For instance, the U.S. Air Force pilot who was shot down behind enemy lines, surviving on bugs and swamp water in Kosovo, was not a hero; the pilots who risked their own necks flying in to save his were.

In our society, we even call football players and Olympic skaters heroes, further confusing the issue. The most you can say for some guy who's looking to win the Super Bowl or a gold medal is that he's a darn good athlete, and leave it at that.

In the main, the 3,000 people who were massacred in Manhattan on September 11, 2001, were no more heroic than you or I. On the other hand, the cops and the firemen, those who ran into the blazing infernos in order to rescue perfect strangers, were the ones who exhibited the requisite bravery and self-sacrifice to deserve the honor.

The point to all this is that you do not turn anyone into a hero simply by calling him one. All you really accomplish is to so totally cheapen the word as to make it meaningless when the real thing comes along.

• 43 •

In Harm's Way

As I recall, Americans began emasculating our armed services during the Gulf War. Understand, I'm not referring to the military's throwing the doors open to women and gays. Anyone who elects to serve his or her country is aces in my book. I refer, instead, to the unseemly coddling of our soldiers. I refer to the insistence by way too many civilians that members of the military never be placed in harm's way. I beg your pardon!

Believe me, please, when I say that I don't wish to see our young people treated as cannon fodder, sacrificed needlessly on foreign battlefields. But that is quite a different matter from swaddling them in baby bunting. They are not porcelain figurines; they are supposed to be America's fighting force.

At what point, I wondered, had we begun to confuse the Army with the Cub Scouts? It seems to have begun, oddly enough, after we went to an all-volunteer military. At least it would have been logical during the time of the draft for friends and relatives to have voiced concern for the comfort and safety of those inducted against their will, the kids who went off kicking and screaming to basic training. But, for a number of years now, the only folks in uniform are those who choose to be.

Now, I realize, of course, that many of the youngsters who enlisted simply joined up in order to get a free education. Which is fine and dandy. But they knew going in that there was a fairly good chance that, along with being all they could be, they just might be called upon to fight for their country. That's the way it works when you sign up with Uncle Sam. Go work for the post office and you have to worry about pit bulls and disgruntled co-workers; go work for the military and you have to worry about the Axis of Evil.

I'm pretty certain that my fellow Americans stopped seeing soldiers as heroic warriors in the John Wayne mode and, thanks perhaps to all those M*A*S*H reruns, saw them as more like Alan Alda, during our first showdown with Saddam Hussein. I still remember the national frenzy when the media reported that the chocolate bars in the G.I. mess kits were melting in Kuwait! The way people carried on, you'd have thought the treads were falling off our tanks and our guns were exploding.

Whereas during World War II, the entire nation mobilized to build planes, buy bonds, and tend Victory Gardens, this time America rolled up its sleeves and came up with a candy bar that could stand up to a blowtorch.

I recall trying to picture Humphrey Bogart, Randolph Scott, or Dana Andrews griping to his Army buddies about the way his Baby Ruth crapped out just when the going got tough on Guadalcanal. I tried, but I failed.

I mean, I think it's fine that we Americans care deeply about our soldiers, sailors and Marines — and that we take it to heart when we get word of casualties. But it's time we quit acting as if these youngsters signed up for summer camp and, through some sort of high level skullduggery, wound up dodging bullets in the Arab desert.

They deserve better than to be patronized. They deserve our respect. And that begins with accepting that in harm's way is just exactly where they're supposed to be.

• 24 •
War: The Ultimate Scapegoat

In the movie *Wall Street,* corporate raider Gordon Gekko announced, "Greed is good." And because Gekko was a villainous character, we knew that Oliver Stone's actual message was that greed is bad.

The truth, of course, is that greed is neither good nor bad. It all depends on the person. For instance, I have no idea if such people as Henry Ford, Thomas Edison, and J.K. Rowling were motivated totally by avarice. What's more, I don't care. In the end, it doesn't matter in the least what prompted their astonishing achievements. What counts is that the world wound up with the electric light, the phonograph, affordable automobiles and a writer who's richer than the Queen of England! — a world unimaginable even to the likes of Jules Verne and H.G. Wells.

Greedy is what other people are; we, ourselves, are merely prudent. Rainy days, after all, have been known to turn into rainy weeks, months, and sometimes years. I suspect that even the likes of Donald Trump and Ted Turner occasionally wonder if they have quite enough cash buried in those coffee cans in the backyard. Another word, like greed, that has an unfortunate reputation is war. The way some people say it, you'd think it was a four-letter word. Over the years, starting in 1930 with *All Quiet on the Western Front,* Hollywood has made a cottage industry out of anti-war movies. Particularly in recent months, it's been impossible to avoid anti-war placards, speeches, and bumper stickers. Well, it's my contention that, just as with greed, it's situational. Sure, sometimes war is awful, but sometimes it's quite wonderful.

Consider a few highlights from our own history. The Revolutionary War gave us liberty from Britain and gave the world democracy. The Civil War preserved the Union and helped end slavery. World War II prevented the barbarians from over-running the earth. Against such magnificent accomplishments as these, peace can't hold a candle.

I realize that some folks are going to bring up innocent bloodshed as an argument against war. But, the truth is that, one way or another, everybody dies. Why is it only a big deal when they die during warfare?

For instance, in America alone, 35,000 people will die this year from influenza; another 50,000 will die in traffic accidents; well over 100,000 will die of tobacco-related diseases. Most of them will perish because they neglected to get flu shots or because they insist on drinking and driving or because they'd rather risk cancer than give up their cigarettes. So, while Americans go nuts every time a soldier dies while doing his duty, you don't see people demonstrating in the streets against the flu, and you don't see Susan Sarandon all over the tube haranguing against booze, and you sure don't see Michael Moore producing message movies about the horrors of nicotine and tars!

The reality is that while bad people — be they Napoleon, Hitler, or Hussein — fight bad wars, good people fight good ones.

• 45 •
Disarming Our Troops

I think that the next person who announces that he opposes the war in Iraq but supports the troops, should be arrested and charged with committing hypocrisy in the first degree.

It has become a mantra with liberals everywhere, but especially with those inside the Beltway. Every Democratic politician can be counted on to say that he hates what our military forces are doing, which, according to Sen. Durbin, includes atrocities the likes of which the world hasn't seen since the days of the Gestapo, but absolutely supports our men and women in uniform.

Have they absolutely no idea how silly and self-serving they sound? They support the troops but despise everything they're doing? They also like to prattle on about how Bush and Rumsfeld are denying the soldiers body armor, ignoring the fact that most of the soldiers in the field don't want to be loaded down with armor because it adds tremendous weight while diminishing their flexibility. I'm reminded that I once heard a sweater described as an article of clothing that kids have to wear when their mothers are cold. I suppose body armor could be described as an article of clothing that soldiers have to wear when guys like Kennedy and Kerry feel a nip in the air.

The liberals also make it a point to ignore the fact that we have an all-volunteer military. They continue to carry on as if the young folks are being carted off, kicking and screaming, from their video games and keg parties.

What liberals cannot bring themselves to accept is that there are young Americans who are proud to serve their country and who, unlike our elected officials, don't require fat salaries, free vacations and mind-boggling pensions in order to do their duty.

It's not just professional politicians who share this cynical attitude. The sons and daughters of liberals also find it impossible to accept that their contemporaries might actually feel moved to make sacrifices for the sake of America.

Liberals see nothing strange about 18-year-olds making career decisions so long as they lead to some money-grubbing profession. But let an 18-year-old decide to enlist in the armed services, and they immediately decide the youngster has been sold a bill of goods by some slick-talking Army recruiter. If the same youngster opts to attend college and major in something as silly as black studies, lesbian studies or 19th century Hungarian poetry, the proud parents mortgage the house and throw a party.

These same liberals are convinced that young soldiers have been abducted by alien creatures, perhaps conservatives from a distant planet, for evil purposes. In other words, they feel the same way that normal people feel when they learn that their sons or daughters have decided to become criminal defense attorneys, so as to devote their lives to defending murderers, rapists, and pedophiles.

But lest you leap to the wrong conclusion, let me hasten to assure you that I fully support all our young, brave, criminal defense attorneys.

Chapter Nine

THE CURSE OF BEING BLACK: HAVING JESSE JACKSON, AL SHARPTON, CHARLES RANGEL, CYNTHIA MCKINNEY, AND LOUIS FARRAKHAN SPEAKING ON YOUR BEHALF

• 46 •

Wanted: Role Models (Only Blacks Need Apply)

Recently, someone asked me who my role models were when I was a kid. Having been a baseball fan all my life and a fairly precocious reader (*The Grapes of Wrath* at age 11), the names I came up with were Ted Williams, Stan Musial, John Steinbeck, William Saroyan, and Humphrey Bogart.

For someone born in Chicago in 1940, but raised in L.A. from the age of six, it wasn't a particularly unusual list, consisting, as it did, of a couple of baseball greats, two very successful California-based writers, and a movie actor who personified cool. What I now find interesting about my list is that not one of those named was Jewish.

It should be stated that none of my friends would have mentioned our dads in this context. A dad, in our neighborhood at least, did not hit home runs or win Pulitzers. But he was our idea of what a grown-up man was supposed to be like, except maybe a little bit thinner and with a lot more hair. Dads were honest, a little bit strict, and definitely people we didn't want to piss off.

I'm not suggesting I hadn't heard of any admirable, high-profile Jews. I was very much aware of boxing great Benny Leonard, football legend Sid Luckman, Hall of Famer Hank Greenberg, and any number of Hollywood luminaries, including John Garfield, Jack Benny, George Burns, Artie Shaw, and Eddie G. Robinson. (I even knew what their original names were!) Understand, I liked them all, but, for me, they didn't represent the very top echelon.

All of my friends, Jewish and gentile alike, were the same. In order for someone to be a sports hero or a pop culture icon, they only had to be great; they didn't have to be Jewish or Catholic or anything, for that matter, but splendid.

When I was a kid, for instance, there was only one real boxing champion, and that was Joe Louis. We may not have paraded, as blacks did in Harlem, when he knocked out Billy Conn or Tony Galento, but we all rooted for the Brown Bomber.

And maybe to Italian-American kids, Joe DiMaggio may have been extra-special, but that didn't stop the rest of us from wanting to grow up to patrol center field the exact same, graceful way the Yankee Clipper did.

So, how is it that black kids can only have other blacks as their role models?

Even when I was a youngster, I would hear that the likes of George Washington Carver, Ralph Bunche, and Marian Anderson were credits to their race, and I would wonder why they weren't simply a credit to the human race. I mean, I never heard anyone suggest that Michelangelo or Shakespeare or Bach or even Stan Musial, for that matter, was a credit to the white race. Granted, Italy, England, Germany, and St. Louis may have taken particular pride in them, but that didn't prevent the rest of us from hailing their talent. Why then are blacks disposed to recognizing only what other blacks do?

I know for a fact that millions of walls in the bedrooms of white American teenagers are adorned with posters of black athletes, rappers, and hip-hoppers. I suspect, and am willing to wager, that there is not a comparable number of walls in black homes covered with posters of white or even Hispanic athletes, movie stars, and musicians.

Let's face it, back in the days when the only things O.J. Simpson was knifing through were defensive lines, his posters were to be found in more bedrooms than Warren Beatty, Wilt Chamberlain and Hugh Hefner put together. O.J. was then supplanted by the omnipresent Michael Jordan.

My question is twofold: One, why should it be that in a society that, ideally, is supposed to be colorblind, black kids are encouraged to recognize human accomplishment only when it's done by people who share their pigmentation? And two: How long will black America turn a blind eye on the sad fact that with a staggering illegitimacy rate of 70%, the only black male role models most of these kids have are those Nike ads taped to their walls?

• 47 •

It's Black and White

Recently, I was being interviewed on radio by a black woman. We were getting along fine until she decided to attack me for suggesting that most of the racists in America are black.

She refuted my conclusion, arguing that even the brouhaha over Janet Jackson's bared breast proved that white America was a racist society.

I couldn't believe my ears. I asked her if she'd been unaware of the stink raised over Britney Spears smooching with Madonna. And that display took place on a music awards show that had nothing like the audience that the Super Bowl commanded.

I told the woman she might as well suggest that the Santa Barbara D.A. was only picking on Janet's brother because he's black, or beige or ash-colored.

Sometimes, it's easy to get the idea that many black Americans are unaware that there are well over 200 million of us who, without being black, garner our share of grief and misery. It goes with being human beings and has nothing to do with pigmentation.

Even the high and mighty aren't above the fray. Go back a few years and you have the spectacle of Richard Nixon's having to resign from the highest office in the land. Or consider V.P. Dan Quayle, who suffered far more public humiliation than Ms. Jackson simply because, one, he forgot how to spell "potatoes," and, two, he voiced a legitimate concern that TV's Murphy Brown was setting a bad example for America's youth by having a child out of wedlock.

People ridiculed Quayle by pointing out that Ms. Brown was a fictional character. But, then, who ever claimed a fictional character couldn't influence the highly impressionable? Look at Huck Finn and Scarlett O'Hara, the Three Musketeers, Rocky Balboa, Superman, and Hillary Clinton.

When Al Campanis and Trent Lott misspoke on the subject of blacks, they were immediately banished to Lower Slobovia. However, lambasting whites is a certain path to success for many upwardly mobile black Americans.

Let Pat Robertson dare run for the presidency and the liberal media castigates him for blurring the division between church and state. But nary a discouraging word is voiced when reverends Jackson and Sharpton toss their hats in the ring. And while we're on the subject, do those two palookas ever bother attending church, let alone ever actually functioning as ministers?

When I suggested to the radio hostess that the biggest problems for blacks in this country were self-inflicted, and that whites were not responsible for a 70% illegitimacy rate, for turf wars over drugs, and for the alarming drop-out rate among high school and college students, she said I simply wouldn't understand — that it was a black thing!

The fact is, most blacks who are raped, robbed, and murdered are the victims, not of white bigots or white cops, but of black thugs.

But some people find it easier to play the race card, to pretend every time black celebrities are arrested it's because rotten white society is out to get them. Funny how that works, though. The same society that arrested O.J. Simpson had first given him a college education and then handed him millions of dollars to play football, make movies, and run through airports in TV commercials.

The very same society that arrested Michael Jackson, Mike Tyson, and Kobe Bryant first made them kazillionaires.

It's the same society that has made icons of Oprah Winfrey, Bill

Cosby, Michael Jordan, Denzel Washington, Halle Berry, Tiger Woods, Quincy Jones, Alice Walker, Toni Morrison, Barry Bonds, Shaquille O'Neal, Colin Powell, and Condoleezza Rice.

If this were a racist society, believe me, we would not know any of those names. Those people would be working in the fields or doing time in the gulags or they'd be dead. That's the way it works in racist societies.

I do not happen to believe that most white Americans in 2006 are bigots. I think, by and large, we judge blacks exactly the way that Dr. King suggested — by their character and their intelligence and their ability. It's the same way we judge each other.

However, we don't have a lot of sympathy for those who claim to be victims of racial oppression. We can't stomach those who wallow in self-pity, demanding everything from reparations to college degrees as birthrights.

We have no patience with those who blame their lack of ambition in school or the workplace on people they don't even know. And we certainly have no use for the creeps who spawn all those millions of children, condemning them to be raised in fatherless homes, simultaneously condemning the rest of us to live with the violent, undisciplined punks so many of them will inevitably grow up to be.

Needless to say, the lady on the radio took strong exception to my words.

I simply couldn't get through to her. It must be a white thing.

• 48 •

"She's Not Heavy, She's My Ho"

Something that is unique among a large segment of America's black population is the use of obscenities when addressing one another. It is odd that the same people who insist on referring to non-relatives as "sister" and "bro" are just as likely to call one another "nigger," "bitch," and "ho."

The same words that would provoke a bloodbath if spoken by a white or Hispanic person allegedly confirms a bond of friendship between the two parties when uttered by blacks.

Although "nigger" is a vile racial epithet, blacks will insist that it is perfectly acceptable so long as they alone bandy it about. How bizarre is that? In my entire life, I have never once heard a Jew refer to himself or his friends as "kikes," "sheenies," or "yids." I always understood that's what you had enemies for.

I do not believe that any Asian would take kindly to being called a "nip," a "chink," or a "slope," no matter what the race or the nationality of the name-caller. If one Italian called another a "wop" or a "dago," I guarantee somebody's nose would be punched. Can you imagine a Puerto Rican calling a friend a "spic" or one Arab referring to his best friend as a "raghead"? No, neither can I.

What the heck is it with American blacks that they, and only they, of all the minorities, perpetuate the vile language of those who most despise them? What other group of Americans demeans its young women as whores with such regularity that their teenage girls refer to themselves and each other as bitches?

And it can't all be the fault of rap and hip hop music, and the crotch-grabbing comics of Def Comedy Jam, as trashy as all that stuff is. If Jesse Jackson really wanted to do something for someone besides himself, he would start hectoring his own people and quit lining his pockets by cashing in on white guilt and white gutlessness.

In spite of what people like Jackson, Waters, and Sharpton may contend to the contrary, the problem for blacks in this country isn't white people. Moreover, it's got nothing to do with what Rush Limbaugh says about a professional quarterback. It has nothing to do with whether or not a black ever gets to manage the New York Yankees. And whether or not blacks are adequately represented in the world of NASCAR is equally inconsequential. Instead, the question all these high-profile blacks should be addressing is this: How it is that, on the one hand, no other minority so incessantly demands respect from everybody else, while at the same time exhibiting so little of it themselves?

• 49 •
Profile This!

When I hear members of the black and Latino communities complain about being profiled by law enforcement, I yawn. What's the big deal? I'm willing to bet that I've been stopped by more cops than 99% of all gang members and 100% of all law-abiding citizens, no matter what color they are.

Now, it's true that, aside from getting my share of traffic tickets, I haven't had too many dealings with the law over the past four decades. But between the time I was 12 and, say, 22, I was probably stopped at least two dozen times.

It all began when my family moved to an apartment that was a block beyond the poor, southern boundary of Beverly Hills. As it happens, I often rode my bicycle into that chi-chi community either to visit one of the two bookstores on little Santa Monica or to practice my set-shot at a Beverly Hills school playground that was about a half mile from my home. I was never surprised — especially when I was pedaling after dark — to be stopped and questioned by a cop. He would ask me where I lived, where I was going, and then call the station to find out if I was wanted for anything. The entire process took about a minute or two.

When I turned 16 and started driving, I continued getting stopped on a regular basis. But now the L.A. cops joined their Beverly Hills brethren in Operation Prelutsky. The problem was that I looked so young that cops spotting me at the wheel of the family car quite naturally took me for a 13-year-old out joyriding. Why anyone, whatever his age, would swipe a seven-year-old Chevy sedan is anybody's guess, but the cops must have assumed that I was not only a thief, but that I had lousy taste in cars.

By the time I was attending college, I had quit driving the Chevy and was riding a motorcycle. On those nights I worked late at the UCLA *Daily Bruin* and would find myself tootling down Sunset after midnight, once again in the domain of the BHPD, I could count on being stopped on a regular basis.

Now that I look back on those years, I may have been stopped as many as twenty or thirty times. And whether or not you choose to believe it, I never took offense. Now, how could it be that I, who had no criminal record, wasn't angry about being stopped and questioned more times than Mickey Cohen and Bugsy Siegel put together? Simple. It's because I agreed with the cops. I *was* a suspicious character. I knew there weren't a lot of kids riding their bikes in Beverly Hills at night. I knew only too well that I looked too young to be legally driving a car. I knew I was the only person riding through Beverly Hills on a motorcycle in the wee hours of the morning. Why on earth wouldn't they stop and question me?

I honestly felt the cops were right. They weren't beating me up or trying to make me confess to unsolved crimes, for crying out loud! They'd ask me who I was and what I was up to, and then, satisfied, they'd send me on my way. I don't recall any of them apologizing for the inconvenience. But why should they? They were earning their salary. It wasn't as if they were warning me never again to ride my bike, car, or motorcycle in their neck of the woods.

In short, if I had been a cop, I would have stopped me. You want to call it profiling, fine; I call it doing their job.

Unless you're some sort of politically correct, lying yahoo, you'll admit that you've seen cars filled with young, sullen-looking blacks, Chicanos, and whites in neighborhoods where they obviously didn't live — and if you'd been a cop, you'd have pulled them over and asked a few questions of your own.

But, then, there are some pinheads nowadays who insist that for every twenty-five-year old Muslim interrogated by airport security, a eighty-year-old granny and a two-year-old toddler should be strip-searched.

In this day and age, when we are told on the one hand that society should be colorblind, but that affirmative action should allow blacks and browns to leapfrog over whites and yellows, clear thinking is the biggest victim of bigotry. It's common sense that's being moved to the back of the bus.

Affirmative action, according to its proponents, is supposed to make up for what white Americans did to black Americans a very long time ago. Well, carried to its logical and obscene extreme, a strong argument could be made for blacks being allowed to have white slaves! And before too long, I fully expect Al Sharpton to make it part of his mantra.

It sounds silly, I know, but how is it any sillier than blacks demanding reparations for slavery? For one thing, the ancestors of most living Americans didn't even come to this country until decades after slavery ended. For another, the number of white Americans who died in the war to end slavery far exceeded the number of whites who owned slaves.

So, possibly, an argument could be made that those blacks who are constantly demanding that America apologize for slavery — without ever taking the Arabs to task for rounding up their ancestors and delivering them to the slave ships — should finally come forward and thank the ancestors of those who died at Shiloh and Bull Run and Gettysburg, for having made the ultimate sacrifice.

• 50 •

Diversity, Schmiversity

A few years ago, I was an executive story consultant on the Dick Van Dyke series, "Diagnosis Murder." A fancy title, but it just meant I was a member of the writing staff.

There were five of us working in the writers room. We were, by most measures, a fairly diverse group of individuals. Two of us were born in New York, one in New Orleans, one in Chicago, one in a small town in Utah. Three of us were Jews, ranging from conservative down to merely cultural; one was an ex-Catholic; one was Mormon.

Four of us were married, one was a confirmed bachelor. Three of us had been married more than once; one of us had been married five times. Between us, we had seven children, one adopted, ranging in age from five to twenty-eight.

Two of us believed in God, one was an atheist, one was agnostic, and one of us suspected that the higher power was none other than Dick Van Dyke.

Two of us believed in capital punishment, two were opposed, one wasn't certain. Three of us were college graduates, two of us weren't. Three of us voted for Gore, one for Bush, one for Nader.

Two of us had been journalists, one of us had been a bartender, one had been a West Point cadet, and one had been an aspiring actress.

Two of us rooted for the Yankees, one for the Red Sox, and two of us thought the other three were nuts for liking baseball.

In my opinion, in spite of the fact that we were all Caucasians, all of us in our fifties, and all of us TV writers, we were as different as a random group of five adult Americans is likely to be.

Hardly a day went by that we weren't arguing about something — and it was only rarely about a story point or a murder clue in one of our scripts.

However, there are those people who would insist that because none of us were black or Hispanic, we couldn't possibly be a model of true diversity in the workplace.

Doesn't it seem peculiar that liberals who are so fond of quoting Dr. Martin Luther King's remark about judging people by their character, not the color of their skin, are the very ones these days who are so totally hung up on pigmentation?

The idea that the folks governing admissions at the University of Michigan would award 20 points (out of a possible 120) to a prospective student for merely being black is simultaneously patronizing and bigoted. After four decades of Head Start programs, court-mandated busing, and billions of dollars earmarked for minority education, black students require 20 points in order to compete?

Doesn't the terrible rate of attrition among black college students suggest that affirmative action isn't such a hot idea? Isn't it just possible that leap-frogging black and Hispanic eighteen-year-olds over the backs of white and Asian students isn't just un-American, but is downright stupid and ill-advised? Reverse bigotry is still bigotry.

As any third grader knows, taking cuts is always unfair, unjust, the rotten act of a schoolyard bully — and it makes no difference if the school is Elm Street Elementary or Harvard.

In all the self-righteous crusading on behalf of student diversity, what I don't hear anyone clamoring for is diversity among the instructors. After all, in the Groves of Academe, especially in the so-called Humanities at the major universities, it would be safe to wager that at least 90% of the faculty members are Democrats. Moreover, I would suggest that liberal bias in the classroom, with all those youngsters soaking up left-wing propaganda and regurgitating it in the form of Blue Book exams, is a far greater menace to a democratic society than a school's failure to meet an arbitrary quota based on ethnicity.

Anyone who thinks the hues of the students are more important than the views of the professors has a badly warped sense of priorities. He is the sort of person who, if he'd been aboard the Titanic, would have still been complaining about the hors d'oeuvres as the ship went down.

• 51 •
Reflections on Reparations

At Louis Farrakhan's recent hate fest in our nation's capital, the bottom-feeders were once again demanding our nation's capital in the form of reparations.

When I first heard blacks talking about these entitlements, I have to admit I started to laugh. Let's face it, it sounded exactly like the sort of get-rich-quick schemes that the Kingfish used to conjure up on "Amos 'n' Andy." And funny as he was, he wasn't half as wacky as Al Sharpton, Jesse Jackson, and Charles Rangel.

We all know there is so much white guilt floating around that if you could only transform it into electrical power, America would be freed of its dependence on fossil fuels. But, come on now. Reparations?!

I recall wondering if I might be missing something. Were these people seriously demanding that damages should be paid 140 years after the end of slavery? What ever happened to the statute of limitations? What ever happened to common sense? And where do people four or five generations after the fact get off demanding payoffs? People who weren't hurt demanding money from people who never hurt anyone? It sounded to me like a whole new definition of chutzpah. Or, if you prefer, like a plank in the Democratic platform.

The more I thought about it, the sillier it sounded. First of all, there's the question of where the money would come from. The answer, obviously, is the same magical place from which all entitlements emanate — the pockets of the middle class taxpayers.

But surely we couldn't all be expected to kick in, could we? After all, surely black Americans couldn't be required to ante up. But, then, neither could most white Americans, whose own ancestors, by and large, didn't arrive on these shores until long after the Civil War had settled the issue once and for all.

And, heaven knows, you couldn't very well demand reparations from those American Yankees whose forefathers not only ran the Underground Railroad, but perished by the tens of thousands in that bloodiest of all wars. In fact, one could make a case that it's blacks who owe a debt to the ancestors of those men who perished at Shiloh and Bull Run and Gettysburg.

Once you get done eliminating innocent parties, who's left to foot the bill? Mainly volunteers, I suspect. People like Kennedy, Boxer, Gore, Kerry, and the Clintons, people in the business of feeling everybody's pain, would be free to pony up for the rest of us. The question would still remain: What do you do about mulattos? Would they only get to collect fifty cents on the dollar?

I'm sure when most people first heard about reparations, they dismissed it as just another of those race-baiting notions that seem to appear with the obnoxious regularity of death, taxes, and a Jesse Jackson photo op. But when I thought about all the Yankee soldiers who died while preserving the Union and ending slavery, it occurred to me that there are millions of us who could line up for a piece of the reparation pie.

For instance, long after blacks left the plantation, the Chinese were brought to America as cheap coolie laborers to lay railroad tracks. And once that job was over, they were treated like curs. By custom and by law, they were restricted to the worst jobs and the worst slums.

Let us not forget women. Once reparations catch on, the ladies will be front and center with their endless list of grievances regarding life as it's lived in a patriarchal society. You think picking cotton was bad? Try packing the kids off to school, picking up the dry cleaning, shopping, driving the tots to their play dates, cooking, cleaning, and holding down a second job, all the while refraining from murdering the slob she's married to who insists on leaving his dirty socks on the floor!

Frankly, if this thing actually gets off the ground, I plan to submit my own claim. I'm short, you see, and in this country that's a far greater handicap than being black, Chinese, or female.

Finally, though, let me say that I agree with the brave black *New York Times* reporter who, a few years ago, wrote that, as abominable as slavery was, he, personally, was grateful that it brought his ancestors to this country, enabling their great-great-great-great-grandson to be born an American.

Chapter Ten

A BIT MORE FLOTSAM

• 52 •

A World Gone Mad

I hope you'll pardon me if I take a moment to suggest that a great many of my fellow Americans are just plain nuts.

In recent weeks, I have had this notion driven home repeatedly. For instance, it seems almost every time I've tuned in ESPN, I have witnessed thousands of San Franciscans give standing ovations to Barry Bonds as he's strolled up to home plate. As bad as that is, I have had people defend him to me on the grounds that it's never been established that he's ever used steroids. Well, even Bonds admits he used products produced in the infamous Balco labs. What he claims is that he had no idea that they could possibly be performance-enhancing drugs. Of course he didn't. He used them because he wanted to turn his head into a pumpkin and become the first player in major league history to wear a size 17 baseball cap!

My second inkling that lunacy is rampant in the land took place in the waiting room of my friendly chiropractor. While waiting for Dr. Ross to make my lower back say, "Uncle!" I sat thumbing through an old copy of *The New Yorker.* Having finally deciphered most of the cartoons, I actually began reading a piece about Sam Alito's upcoming confirmation hearing. (I told you it was an old copy.) Suddenly, in the middle of the article, I came across one of those lines that seemed so wacky, I figured I had misread it. So I backed up and tried it a second time, only to confirm that the problem wasn't with me, but with Jeffrey Toobin, who wrote the following: "If Anthony M. Kennedy, David H. Souter, Ruth Bader Ginsburg, and Stephen Breyer had forthrightly answered questions about their judicial philosophies, they almost certainly would have been confirmed anyway; all of them belong in the large middle ground of American politics."

It is such an outlandish statement that it hardly merits comment except to point out that these are four of the five nincompoops who voted the wrong way in this year's infamous eminent domain case, and that Mrs. Ginsburg, in her former life, was chief counsel for the ACLU. However, in the rarified atmosphere in which *New Yorker* writers and readers reside, this is regarded as middle of the road. Believe me, by the time Dr. Ross had me on the table, both my back and my brain were in spasm.

But I was in for even more craziness after I wrote a piece in which I suggested that, for all their faults, Republican politicians were better than Democrats, and that conservatives who stayed home in November or vented their anger by voting for third party candidates ran the very real risk of shooting themselves in the foot.

I heard from hordes of disgruntled right-wingers, many of whom had the effrontery to accuse me of being (naïve) (stupid) (a liberal) (John McCain's stooge) (all of the above).

As usual, I made it a point to reply to each of my critics, but I have to assume there were others who were simply too lazy to write or were willing to give me the benefit of the doubt. So I will take this opportunity to try to set the record straight.

I share the frustration of my fellow conservatives. I, too, have become increasingly disillusioned, not just with the president, but with his Republican cohorts in the Capitol. They have squandered a golden opportunity to use their clout to effect real change in Washington. To many of us, they seem to have spent far more time trying to curry favor with Democrats than to promote a conservative agenda. Instead of behaving like the guys in control of the Oval Office and both houses of Congress, they've been mincing around like palace eunuchs frightened to death of offending the resident caliph.

The problem is that, all that being said, the Democrats are even worse. Sending a message to the GOP in 2006 by sitting out the election means putting liberals at the wheel. These lefties are dangerous enough when they're merely backseat drivers.

A third party would be made up of right-wing dissidents, thus splitting the ranks of the Republicans and ensuring that Senator Clinton gets to return to the White House, and not just on a visitor's pass.

Sending a message to the Republican politicians by voting the incumbents out of office will simply result in their having to change careers, thus creating a glut of high-priced lobbyists. Big deal! It's we, the people, who will have to suffer the dire consequences.

How's this for a nightmare scenario? The year is 2009. The cast of characters includes President Hillary Rodham Clinton, Secretary of State Ted Kennedy, Secretary of Defense John Kerry, Attorney General Al Gore, Senate Majority Leader Harry Reid, House Majority Leader Nancy Pelosi, Supreme Court Justice Bill Clinton, and Senate Sergeant-At-Arms Cynthia McKinney.

All you right-wingers who are seriously considering staying home in November or squandering your votes on third party nonentities should stop and consider the possible ramifications of your self-indulgent mischief.

But it's a matter of principle, you say. We've got to do what we've got to do, you insist. What have we got to lose? Let's just try it and see. What's the worst that could happen?

The last person who said all those things, let me remind you, was Dr. Frankenstein.

· 53 ·
It's Time to Evict the U.N.

My wife would like to see us kick the United Nations out of the United States. I, for one, think it's a swell idea. What's more, I'm certain that most New Yorkers feel the same. After all, for the past 58 years, the gang of scofflaws has taken advantage of their diplomatic immunity to be the worst kind of guests. Double-parking is the least of it.

Probably the only people who would miss these expense account spongers are the waiters and maitre d's at the more expensive Manhattan eateries.

My own reason for wanting the U.N. padlocked is that I object to corruption and hypocrisy being passed off as high mindedness. I heard rumors that Kofi Annan, which sounds like a twelve-step program for caffeine addicts, collected a nice piece of change out of Iraq's phony oil-for-food program. But my problem with the organization is more basic than that, although it does explain how it is that Mr. Annan seems to have a more extensive, more expensive wardrobe than Donald Trump.

People such as John Kerry are always eager to get the U.N.'s good housekeeping seal of approval before America makes a foreign policy decision. Or at least Kerry and company do when there's a Republican in the White House. I don't seem to recall its having been quite so imperative when Clinton and Lewinsky were holding down the Oval Office. Be that as it may, what nation in its right mind would surrender even a scintilla of its sovereignty to a group as loathsome as the member states of the U.N.? I would sooner trust the Mafia to call the shots. You think I'm indulging in hyperbole? At least I have no reason to think that, for all their faults, the Cosa Nostra hates America. I mean, consider that among the regimes having votes are the likes of Cuba, China, the Democratic People's Republic of Korea (North Korea to you), Laos, Cambodia, Rwanda, Myanmar, Sudan, Uganda, and two dozen Muslim-dominated dictatorships running the gamut from Bahrain to Yemen. And that's not even counting France. Understand, the U.N., while going ballistic over America's rescuing Iraq from Saddam Hussein's iron grip, did nothing about genocide in Rwanda and the Sudan. The U.N., while taking every opportunity to chastise Israel, treated Yasser Arafat as if he were another Mother Teresa and his gang of suicide bombers were just so many good Samaritans going about their business. But even aside from all that, I counted 33 member nations with populations under 1,000,000. In fact, there are a baker's dozen with populations under 100,000! We don't call places that size countries, we call them counties or neighborhoods. The total population of those 33 countries, ranging alphabetically from Andorra (67,509) to San Marino (24,521), is slightly in excess of 10 million, the same as Seoul, Korea, for crying out loud! If you can believe it, there are only 16,952 people in Palau. Palau has a seat in the United Nations, and, what's more, their ambassador can park anywhere he damn well pleases! It so happens Palau is a true ally of America's, but do you really want, say, San Marino having a say in matters of American foreign policy? On top of all that, the U.S. not only pays most of the freight for the U.N., but we don't even charge them rent. Can you imagine what someone like Trump would pay for that piece of real estate?

So, give me one good reason why these good-for-nothing freeloaders shouldn't be sent packing. Let them set up camp in the Hague or Geneva or Fallujah, for that matter.

If anyone feels the absolute need for America to belong to a fraternal organization, I would suggest something smaller and a tad more selective, something like the Elks or a summer bowling league.

• 54 •
Gripes and Grievances

"It was the best of times, it was the worst of times," wrote Charles Dickens, back in 1859. Well, here it is 2006, and I'd say his words are as accurate today as the day he wrote them. For some people, this is the best time to be alive, while, for others, it's the pits. But for still other people, such as myself, it is, as usual, a matter of trying to uncover a bit of sanity midst all the chaos. Believe me, it's like panning for gold in the gutter.

I'm reminded that when Irving Thalberg brought the Marx Brothers to MGM, he told Groucho that the reason their Paramount movies, such as *Cocoanuts* and *Animal Crackers,* hadn't done well was because there was no let-up to the Marxian madness. Thalberg said that the audience needed a few breaks along the way. It was at Thalberg's insistence that romantic subplots and musical interludes be interspersed with the hijinks. The result was that movies such as *A Night at the Opera* and *A Day at the Races* actually made money.

Well, that's exactly what I need — a few breaks in the madness. In a world in which Rep. Cynthia McKinney can behave like a spoiled brat and paint herself as an innocent victim, I can do with a few musical interludes myself. McKinney, who has been elected to six terms in the House of Representatives for no better reason than that she has constituents who are even dumber than she is, wasted no time sharing photo ops with every left-wing black celebrity in America, from Harry Belafonte to Danny Glover. For good measure, instead of simply apologizing to the guard who was merely doing his thankless job, she dealt the race card from the bottom of the deck, demanding that he be fired.

That reminds me how the whole matter of equality in this country has been turned on its head. Whenever I hear about any group, be they blacks, Latinos, gays, or lesbians, asking to be treated equally, I just about gag. We all know that groups of any stripe don't ever want to be treated as equals; instead, they want and demand special treatment. For no other reason than that they are members of this group, they feel they're unique and, therefore, entitled. What's more, they don't have to do anything in order to prove how extraordinary they are. They merely have to have a certain pigmentation or share a certain sexual proclivity. And, best of all, they don't have to attend meetings or pay monthly dues.

Next, I'm annoyed by handicapped parking spaces. Now, understand, I don't object to a few set-asides. What I do object to is that every other person seems to have a handicap sign on his windshield. Few things get me so riled up as driving round and round a parking lot while some joker who walks every bit as well as I do pulls into one of those spaces and then strolls away. If the person driving the car doesn't get into a wheelchair, I say he should wind up in one!

Speaking of people getting away with stuff, if the Constitution prevents our deporting the corporate CEOs who out-source the jobs of hard-working Americans, the least we should do is publicize who these traitors are, so that decent people can shun them. A good start would be putting their faces on milk cartons and beer cans. If it were up to me, I'd put a scarlet G, for greedy, on their foreheads. Surely I can't be the only person who thinks there should be a very real downside to downsizing.

Can we all agree that it is the height of hypocrisy when Democrats, who quickly attack right-wing clergy for speaking out on abortion or any other issue of public concern, keep their yaps zipped up tight when ministers such as Al Sharpton and Jesse

Jackson run for president? And I have yet to hear a single liberal take L.A.'s pedophile-protecting Cardinal Mahoney to task for being such a cheerleader for illegal immigration.

Finally, I'm wondering if I'm the only person who was surprised that scientists recently discovered the fossil of a strange fish-like creature they claim first crawled onto dry land about 375 million years ago. They're calling it for reasons of their own the *Tiktaalik roseae,* and claiming it's the missing link between fish and humans. I don't mind telling you that the discovery cost me a pretty penny. In the office pool, my money was riding on Al Gore.

Now, do you better understand why I wish there were a break in the lunacy, and Tony Martin or Allan Jones would break into song?

· 55 ·

Just Call Me "Rip Van Prelutsky"

Occasionally, I find myself feeling like a modern-day Rip Van Winkle. It sometimes seems as if, overnight, while I've been snoozing, the rest of the world has glommed onto something like a pit bull with a lamb chop.

For instance, take the word "Oriental." I had always used that word to mean people and things whose origin was the Far East. And while I used it to denote people whose skin was yellow, I never regarded it as a pejorative. The fact is, I never heard anybody use the word in a derogatory fashion.

That is not to suggest that I was unaware of all the hatred directed at Orientals. Going back to the days of the coolies who laid railroad tracks across this country, they have had to deal with open hostility. And things certainly didn't improve once we waged war in short order against Japan and North Korea. However, bigots never referred to the enemy as Orientals. Instead, their vulgar vocabulary consisted of Jap, slope, slant, Nip, Chink, and gook.

In my experience, nobody ever said "Oriental" and meant anything bad by it. In fact, when coupled with rugs, painting and cuisine, it invariably indicated something terrific. But, one day, I awoke and discovered that the PC police had decided that we were all supposed to lump yellow people and brown people together and call the end-result Asians.

A year or so ago, I asked a friend, a Nisei, just when the word had come to have a negative connotation. He admitted that he had no idea. Moreover, neither he nor anyone he knew had ever regarded it as an insult.

Yet another example of something that the rest of you seem to have decided while I was busy napping is that the reason minority kids are doomed to failure is because they're raised in slums and ghettos.

I have a major problem with that notion. For well over a hundred years, immigrants from Germany, Russia, Poland, Greece, Hungary, Italy, China, Scandinavia, etc., flooded into America — most of them poor, uneducated, unable to speak English — but it was a given that they, and especially their children, would be motivated by their circumstances to achieve success through education and hard work.

But, somewhere along the way, no doubt while I was catching forty winks, liberals turned that notion on its head. Today, when so many minority youngsters turn to drugs, gangs, and teenage promiscuity, the reason for it, according to Hillary Clinton and *The New York Times,* is invariably that old standby, poverty.

The problem is that it only seems to have that detrimental effect on blacks and Hispanics. For every other group, oddly enough, poverty appears to be as large a stick as it ever was, and the American dream remains the biggest carrot mankind has ever known.

• 56 •

Guns and Sons of Guns

I have a terrible confession to make. You see, even though I am not a hunter, never really considered Charlton Heston a very good actor, and only recently joined the NRA — mainly so I could wear their cap and annoy my liberal acquaintances — I have no objection to my fellow citizens owning guns.

Understand, I am referring to decent, law-abiding people who realize that this is a rather violent society and that the police can't be everywhere at once. Without weapons, how are people supposed to protect themselves from rapists, killers, and home invaders?

With a kazillion guns already in circulation, Brady Bill or no Brady Bill, I'm afraid we'll never again see the day that criminals have to make do with rocks and sharp sticks.

Oddly enough, it's often the very same people who get irate about their neighbors having the means to defend themselves who are the folks most opposed to mandatory sentences for gun-toting felons. It's as if they're against the possession of guns by amateurs, but hate the idea of denying professionals the necessary tools of their trade.

However politically correct one chooses to be, the fact remains that in those states where people are allowed to carry weapons, crime statistics plummet. And for once, statistics are borne out by common sense. After all, if you're a punk looking to mug someone, it figures you'll think twice if there's a good chance your intended victim is better armed than you.

But where guns are concerned, statistics and common sense rarely have the power to sway a liberal's opinion. They simply won't accept the idea that guns are ever used defensively to safeguard the innocent. So far as they're concerned, the Founding Fathers were all drunk the day they drafted that part of the Bill of Rights having to do with bearing arms.

In terms of public relations, I think it would be wise if just once, when some kid blasts a schoolmate, Michael Moore and the rest of the anti-gun crowd didn't take such obvious delight in using the incident to beat the opposition over the head. In a nation of 300 million people, probably close to 10% of whom are here illegally, bad stuff is going to happen. It's a rotten shame, but it's unavoidable. Believe me, schoolyard bullies and math exams are a far bigger source of terror to most of our kids. There is conclusive proof that the anti-gun zealots are less concerned with the safety of young people than they are with their own holy mission; otherwise, they would put guns on the back burner and concentrate, instead, on getting teenagers off the road. In a country where millions of adolescents are encouraged to start driving cars — cars fueled by a deadly mixture of gasoline and high-octane hormones — one can only laugh at the anti-gun crowd's pretense that public safety is their number one priority.

The battle, for the most part, comes down to liberals vs. conservatives. As usual, liberals turn their backs on common sense, preferring to appear compassionate.

Because they are stuck with an agenda, liberals are forced to parrot anti-gun propaganda even when, like the late columnist Carl Rowan and Sen. Dianne Feinstein, they, themselves, are discovered to be packing heat. And surely I wasn't the only person who yawned when Sharon Stone made such a big deal out of turning in her three roscoes. The point might have been made more forcefully if her bodyguards had turned in their artillery.

Do I think everyone should have a gun? Of course not. But is that something that keeps me up nights? Hardly.

Of far greater concern to me are the yahoos driving around in those lethal, oversized, gas-guzzling, lane-straddling sport-utility vehicles. Armed with a feisty attitude and a few tons of steel, every soccer mom has become a full-fledged menace to society. I swear, there are more tanks to be found in the parking lot at the local supermarket than Gen. George Patton had to face during the entire North African campaign.

• 57 •

101 People Who Are Screwing Up America

Although we have never met, I regard Bernard Goldberg as a friend. He's sent me his books, nicely dedicated; I've sent him mine. Through our frequent exchange of e-mails, I have found that he and I tend to see eye to eye on just about everything. Our chief difference, aside from the fact that I live in L.A. and he lives in Miami, is that while I play tennis, he courts serious injury playing basketball.

When I heard the title of his latest work, I figured it would provide the acid test. After all, when you go and call a book *100 People Who Are Screwing Up America,* one can hardly assume that anybody is going to agree with all your choices. Well, it so happens I do!

Now, some of the names are obvious. In fact they were so obvious that before I even opened the book, I was kicking myself for not having written it. But the truth is, if I had gotten there first, the title would probably have been *The 17 People Who Are Screwing Up America,* and let's face it, nobody's going to fork over $25.95 for a 50-page book.

Where Mr. Goldberg has it all over me is that he obviously takes notes. When some jerk does something really dumb or awful — unless he's somebody famous like Robert Byrd, David Duke, Howard Dean or Al Sharpton — I tend to forget his name after a day or two. As a result, while reading the book, I kept being reminded of nuisances who had slipped off my radar. I refer to people such as

Michael Newdow, the anti-religious zealot who literally made a federal case out of "under God" in the Pledge of Allegiance; Jeff Danziger, the political cartoonist who kept his job and his liberal creds in spite of portraying Condoleezza Rice as an Aunt Jemima; and Nancy Hopkins, who stomped out of a conference and initiated a public lynching of Harvard President Lawrence Summers, all because he had the temerity to wonder whether there might be innate differences between the sexes when it came to science and math.

For the record, Goldberg's top six pains in the neck are Jimmy Carter; the ACLU's national director Anthony Romero; Jesse Jackson; Ted Kennedy; *New York Times* publisher Arthur Sulzberger; and, number one, Michael Moore.

At the end of the book, my friend Bernie invites readers to come up with their own nominees. He now reports that the names that have come up most frequently are Senator Dick Durbin, the idiot who compared our soldiers at Guantanamo to Nazis and other vermin; and the five justices of the Supreme Court who cast the deciding votes in the eminent domain case.

I can't argue against those six candidates making it into Goldberg's sequel. But I had already e-mailed him my own choice. That would be Lorne Michaels. He's the fellow who created "Saturday Night Live" for NBC. At one fell swoop, he not only introduced badly written sketch comedy to a medium that had managed to reach the unimaginable heights of "Your Show of Shows" and "Caesar's Hour," but he also helped to bring movie comedies to their knees. Because he unleashed people like Chevy Chase, Dan Aykroyd, the Belushi brothers, Joe Piscopo, Eddie Murphy, Julia Sweeney, Damon Wayans, Chris Farley, Adam Sandler, Rob Schneider, Janeane Garofalo, and Will Ferrell on Hollywood, I hold him responsible for just about every lousy comedy produced over the past quarter century.

In addition to all the tripe his charges have gone off and done with others, consider the movies he has personally produced. They include *Nothing Lasts Forever, Coneheads, Stuart Saves His Family, Tommy Boy, Black Sheep, The Ladies Man, Superstar, A Night at the Roxbury* and *Brain Candy*. It sounds like half the items in the remainder bin at your neighborhood Blockbuster. It's no wonder that even after all these years of overseeing the sophomoric "SNL," Mr. Michaels has not given up his day job.

In spite of all that, I might have forgiven him everything for the sake of *Groundhog Day,* which he had nothing to do with, but which did star "SNL" alum, Bill Murray.

I might have if it weren't for the fact that back in 1979, Michaels gave Al Franken a national platform. For that, alone, the man should be forgiven nothing.

· 58 ·
Denying the Holocaust

Not too long ago, David Irving was sentenced to three years in an Austrian jail for claiming that the Holocaust never happened. Although I am usually in favor of harsh sentences even for those people who insist on honking their car horns while driving through tunnels, I was against throwing Irving's butt in the slammer.

For some time now, the shmoe has made his living by writing and speaking on the subject. One of his goonier notions is that the concentration camps were erected after the end of World War II to serve as tourist attractions. Irving isn't the only person in the world who insists that the Holocaust was a scheme promoted by Jews in order to extort reparations from the Germans, but I do believe he is the only jackass I've ever heard suggest that it was Poland's plan to build a theme park and call it Auschwitz.

The reason I was sorry to see Irving sent off to jail is because I think people should have the right to make stupid, even offensive remarks. Otherwise, to be consistent, I would want to see Harry Belafonte prosecuted for embracing Hugo Chavez and for telling the Venezuelan crowds that George W. Bush is the worst villain in the world and that America is a terrorist state.

The oddest thing about Holocaust deniers is that, down deep, people like Irving and Iran's Mahmoud Ahmadinejad only wish that Hitler had finished what he started. I guess you could say that the main difference between an anti-Semitic optimist and an anti-Semitic pessimist is whether he views six million dead Jews as a job half-fulfilled or half-unfulfilled.

One of the things I object to about Holocaust deniers is the term itself. It sounds rather impressive, even distinguished. It sort of lends intellectual legitimacy to a bunch of lunatics. It would be like describing people who believe the world is flat as level-headed eartharians or referring to those who are convinced the moon is made of cheese as edamologists.

It also annoys me when seemingly rational people engage these bigoted pinheads in debates on college campuses. Once again, it lends credence to their contention that the Nazis didn't exterminate millions of European Jews. It simply makes no sense to stage a debate with some booby who insists that a ton of photographs, Nazi crematoriums, eyewitness testimony, and Elie Wiesel's books are all part of a gigantic Zionist conspiracy. You might as well hire a hall in order to argue with some yutz who insists that the sun rises in the west and sets in the east. All you're really doing is suggesting that there are two sides to the question and that reasonable people can agree to disagree.

The way I see it, if somebody tells you he's Napoleon Bonaparte, clearly he's insane. However, if you insist in arguing with him, it only goes to prove that you're crazy, too.

• 59 •
Not So Sweet Charity

Not too long ago, I had an argument regarding charity. My friend was of the opinion, shared by many, that one's contributions should always be given anonymously. In other words, it should be a secret shared only with God and, I assume, that granter of tax deductions — the I.R.S.

By their nature, most charitable contributions are anonymous. We send a check to a charity and they, in turn, dispense the funds as they see fit. However, when people give in a more direct fashion, I believe the recipients should know the identities of their benefactors. I believe it's important, not so much in order to receive thanks, but to be in a position to give thanks. There is little enough genuine gratitude in the world without going out of one's way to diminish the small amount that exists.

Frankly, I don't like charitable donations when I don't know exactly who's going to wind up receiving it. While I did write a check after the tsunami hit Indonesia and another when Katrina struck New Orleans, I sent the money to children's charities. I figured that, no matter what sort of parents they might be saddled with, little kids were my idea of innocent victims.

Some of you are probably shocked and dismayed that I don't feel any obligation to lend a helping hand to every last victim of a natural disaster. Some people, to my way of thinking, simply have it coming.

I recall that Alfred P. Doolittle, the father of Eliza, argued in
Pygmalion and, later, in *My Fair Lady,* that the undeserving poor
deserved to receive their fair share of the pie that society was always
prepared to dole out to the deserving poor. In making his case to
Professor Higgins, he pointed out that even ne'er-do-wells such as
himself had to have clothing and food every bit as much as the good
folks, and even more than them when it came to drink!

Here in America, Doolittle would be preaching to the choir.
Poverty in this country isn't a condition, it's an industry. Not only
are there charitable organizations staffed by those to whom it's a lifetime career, but, without the terminally impoverished, many politicians would have nothing to talk about. Without those perennial
"victims," one of the two parties would have gone the way of the
Whigs long before now.

The truth is, there is nothing sacred about being poor. In a land
with as much opportunity as America offers, it's virtually impossible
for a person of average intelligence and even a modicum of ambition
to remain poverty-stricken.

In the old days, in the Windy City where I was born, ward heel-
ers used to pay folks a few bucks apiece to vote at election time.
These days, between welfare handouts, subsidized housing, and
food stamps, the only difference between then and now is that the
practice is no longer limited to Chicago, and the price of a vote has
gone through the roof.

There is an underclass in America consisting of both blacks and
whites that, I'm afraid, has been sold a bill of goods by liberals —
and that's the belief that being poor, lazy, and uneducated constitutes
an occupation for which they are entitled to be paid.

• 60 •

Squaring Accounts

No matter where a discussion about fiscal matters begins — whether the subject involves national defense, farm subsidies, or Social Security — inevitably it ends up with somebody insisting that it's wrong to saddle our sons and daughters with a load of IOUs. Well, I beg to differ.

Inasmuch as I have a son, I feel I have as much right to voice an objection as any other parent, and it's my honest opinion that if I leave him his fair share of the national debt to deal with, it's not the worst thing in the world.

After all, aggravation and worry aside, just look at what he's cost me over the years. I'm not saying I kept track of every last nickel and dime I spent on him, but, believe me, it was a bloody fortune. There were the regular items, of course, such as food and drink, clothes and shelter, schooling and medical expenses. But, like most kids of his generation, there were also those other items he couldn't live without — the pricey PlayStations, the fancy bikes, and the name-brand sneakers that cost more than all the shoes in my closet.

I'm not saying I begrudge him. Well, maybe I am. But not totally. After all, it's not as if he put a gun to my head to get all that stuff. But I must confess that when I'm writing checks these days for the mortgage, water and power, and car insurance I find myself getting misty-eyed over some of that long-gone green.

Although studies indicate that married people live longer than single people, I'm not at all sure that adding children to the mix doesn't merely make life seem longer. Their music alone is enough to drive adults to an early grave.

When you get right down to it, our offspring have a pretty swell deal going for themselves. Not only do they get to shorten our lives, but they then get to inherit our homes, our money, and all our worldly possessions.

So, if the worst thing you can say about space exploration, invading Iraq, or the president's plan to revamp Social Security is that it's going to cost our kids money somewhere down the line, I merely shrug and say, So what? What's the big deal? The bottom line, ladies and gentlemen, is that it's mostly our money they're going to be spending!

• 61 •

Thank You, Andrew Carnegie

I was about eleven years old when I first fell in love with a public library. Up until then, I had certainly been aware that they existed, even apart from the small one at my school, but they had nothing to do with me. At that tender age, however, I happened to read John Steinbeck's *The Grapes of Wrath,* and that literally changed my life.

From that point on, I was never to see one of those little brick buildings without experiencing a sense of wonder and amazement. Say what you will about the human race, any species that can come up with something as magnificent as the library isn't totally worthless. There are very few things, and none that come readily to mind, that compare to them. Artichokes are pretty good, but they're a hell of a lot of work. Sunsets are nice, but they're unreliable. Puppies are cute, but they make a mess. But, where public libraries are concerned, there's simply no downside.

A library card combines all the best attributes of a passport and a genie's lamp. For openers, librarians are unfailingly kind and helpful. If they weren't, considering the pittance they're paid, they'd have gone into some other line of work, such as being meter maids or clerks at the DMV.

For another thing, libraries, themselves, are convenient and trouble-free. It's not just that they're usually within walking distance of your home, either; if one branch doesn't have the book you want, they'll quickly get it from a different branch and hold it for you. If you don't think that's a big deal, I guess you've never tried returning a movie to a different Blockbuster.

On top of everything else, it's all free. The only time a library costs you even a dime is when you neglect to return books or tapes on time. And even then, the cost is so nominal that the obvious purpose of the fine is to remind us to do the considerate thing next time, not to punish us for having been thoughtless this time around.

Andrew Carnegie, born into a poor Scottish family, is a special hero of mine, and not only because he was short. He once wrote, "A man who dies rich, dies disgraced." And so, in the final years of his life, he gave away a third of a billion dollars to good causes, with about twenty percent going to Britain and the rest to his adopted country, America. A part of that generous legacy was the endowment of nearly 3,000 libraries across the United States. Talk about a gift that keeps on giving.

If it were up to me, his would be the fifth head up there on Mt. Rushmore and his birthday, November 25, would be a national holiday.

I regret that I can never hope to repay the debt of gratitude I owe the man. I can only say, thank you, Mr. Carnegie. For owing to your beneficence, from the first time I stepped foot in a public library, I knew I wouldn't have to die to get to heaven.

Chapter Eleven

IN A CERTAIN LIGHT,
THE FOURTH ESTATE
LOOKS LIKE A FIFTH COLUMN

· 62 ·

Have You Ever Noticed That Rooney Rhymes with Goony?

Seeing as how I am one of the plaintiffs in a class action lawsuit targeting several Hollywood entities — studios, networks, and talent agencies — for engaging in discriminatory practices against older writers, I'd have to be the worst sort of rat to suggest that it's high time that CBS sent Andy Rooney packing. So I won't suggest they retire him because he's old. Instead, I'll suggest they give him his gold watch because he's really stupid.

Clearly, in Rooney's case, it isn't a matter of age. His little screeds on "60 Minutes" have been boring and embarrassing for many years. Oddly enough, when I used to watch the show regularly, I didn't notice it quite so much. I sort of got used to how truly awful he was. It's sort of like living with a harmless, but nevertheless crazy, relative. When you're around him all the time, you get used to his shenanigans. But go away for a while and then come back, and the fact that Uncle Sid shoves mashed potatoes in his ears will hit you like a ton of bricks.

So it is with Uncle Andy. Recently, after not having watched "60 Minutes" for a couple of months, I tuned in. By the time 8 p.m. finally rolled around, I found myself wondering if anyone at CBS is paying any attention to Rooney's commentaries.

He began by admitting that he, whom we all know to be a millionaire, drives 20 miles into New Jersey to buy gas because their state tax is slightly lower than New York's, and then wondered, as he chuckled, whether he was actually saving any money.

Bad enough, but it got worse. He went on to insist that the rest of us should all vow to drive 20% less so that we wouldn't have to make "a mess in Alaska."

The real mess is obviously between Rooney's ears.

Every single time this loon fills up his gas tank, he's driving an extra 40 miles to save a few pennies, but the rest of us are supposed to stop driving to the supermarket?!

All of which only proves once again that there's no self-righteous bozo like a wealthy, self-righteous, liberal bozo.

And to prove that this has absolutely nothing to do with age, when Andy Rooney, 86, is retired to pasture, I very much want him to take Lesley Stahl, a mere child of 64, along for company.

• 63 •
All the News that Fits

Only a dyed-in-the-wool leftist would think to label CNN, MSNBC, *The New York Times,* the *Washington Post,* and the three major networks as the mainstream media. Only liberals who are so delusional as to regard their politics as middle-of-the-road could be that mistaken. Normal people are aware of the fact that these news outlets are not only not mainstream, but are clear out of the water and perched on the far left bank of that particular body of water. However, those of the liberal persuasion have repeated that lie so often and for so long, I'm afraid they've actually come to take it as gospel.

Another lie they have attempted to foist on us is that Fox News acts as the propaganda arm of the Republican party. In spite of the fact that Bill O'Reilly has taken the president out behind the woodshed on any number of occasions — taking him to task for his border policy, for expanding the size of the federal government, for increasing the national deficit, and for the port deal with the UAE, to name just a few — the left would have you believe that O'Reilly is Goebbels to Bush's Hitler.

The fact is, it's radio and TV shows moderated by the sorry likes of Al Franken and Chris Matthews that regularly take cheap shots at conservatives, and do so with absolute impunity. They rarely, if ever, give the other side the opportunity to rebut their sophomoric drivel.

O'Reilly may be an acquired taste, but he not only makes it a regular practice to invite the opposition on his show to argue the issues, but invariably ends the debate by giving his guest the last word, closing with his signature line, "We'll let the folks at home decide."

Further proof that Fox plays it on the square is the show that follows on the heels of O'Reilly's. I refer to Hannity and Colmes. While it's certainly true that Hannity is a devout Republican partisan, Colmes is equally devoted to the Democrats. In fact, if Howard Dean ever develops terminal laryngitis from all that infernal screaming, Colmes could easily step in and take over as head of the DNC.

I am not, it should be understood, a cheerleader for Fox's entire lineup. I find Shepard Smith's voice annoying even if I'm in the next room. And I, personally, would relegate Greta Van Susteren and her murders *au jour* to mid-afternoon, where she could duke it out with the likes of Judge Judy and Jerry Springer.

But facts are facts, and the fact is, Fox makes every attempt to live up to its motto of Fair and Balanced. Compared to Fox, the so-called mainstream media is what I'd call Faux News.

• 64 •

Tonight: TV's Worst Interviewer ... Tick, Tick, Tick

When it comes to "60 Minutes," I'm not the only person who suggests it's high time they put Andy Rooney out to pasture. While I will readily admit that I find his whiny, nasal voice almost as annoying as Bob Dylan's, and that I start to get a migraine as soon as I hear him say, "Have you ever noticed...," it's Ed Bradley I'd first send packing if I were running CBS.

My friends will think I am biased against Mr. Bradley because, in his mid-60s, he's still trying to look hip by wearing one of those silly studs in his ear. Not so. While it is true that I don't like that particular affectation any more than I do ponytails on bald men, goatees on baseball players or pinky rings on anybody, the earring, in his case, is the least of it.

My problem with Bradley is that he is forever doing stories about wildly successful black Americans like himself, and instead of celebrating their accomplishments, he invariably portrays them as victims, playing the race card for all it's worth.

For instance, when he did a segment on the legendary Lena Horne, instead of trumpeting a singing career that was still going strong in her 80s and a bi-racial marriage that had endured for decades, Bradley concentrated on her humble origins and her bitterness over Louis B. Mayer's not having turned her into another Ava Gardner.

When Bradley interviewed Ray Charles, did he focus on the

man's fabulous career? Of course not. Instead, at one point, he asked Mr. Charles how much money he was worth, and the singer, too much the gentleman to tell him it was none of his beeswax, replied, "About thirty-five million dollars."

Now, if I'd been interviewing the man, I'd have probably slapped my forehead and said, "Holy Magoly!" But Bradley merely furrowed his brow, shook his head in that patented woe-is-me way of his, and opined, "Not bad, but don't you think you would have made a lot more if you'd been white?"

And Ray Charles, to his discredit, reckoned he would have.

Oh, really? Well, I venture he would have made a lot more if he'd been Michael Jordan or Diana Ross or Michael Jackson or Berry Gordy or Oprah Winfrey or Barry Bonds or Bill Cosby. But I'd like Ed Bradley to show me a blind, *white* blues singer who's got that many zeroes in his bank account.

I suppose we should all be grateful that Mr. Charles wasn't encouraged to whine about Louis B. Mayer's not having turned *him* into another Ava Gardner.

Bradley even managed to pull out the crying towel for his interview with Denzel Washington. I honestly figured that not even he would be able to turn a good-looking, happily married, two-time Oscar winner, currently pulling down $20 million a picture, into a poor, downtrodden wretch. Which only serves me right for underestimating the combined chutzpah of a professional sob sister and a Hollywood movie star.

Because Washington had grown up in an affluent section of New York, a child of privilege, Bradley couldn't indulge in his predictable stroll down mean streets or dusty roads. Instead, he took Mr. Washington back to visit his prep school, so that the actor could get misty-eyed while pointing out the spot — yes, the exact spot, as if it had historical importance — where Denzel's mother had broken the news that she and his father were getting a divorce!

As Bradley's colleague would say, "Have you ever noticed how people are always making fun of the way Larry King and Barbara Walters conduct their interviews, but nobody ever says anything about the way the old guy with the fercocktah earring conducts his?"

Chapter Twelve

THOSE WHO CAN, TEACH; THOSE WHO CAN INDOCTRINATE, GET TENURE

• 65 •
The Dumbing Down of Academe

Just when you think the folks on the left can't get any goofier, they go and surpass themselves. If silliness were an Olympic event, these lunkheads could be counted on to bring home the gold. The fool's gold, that is.

Actually, they could probably excel in the sprints, seeing as how they're not weighed down with a whole lot of common sense.

In case you haven't gotten the word, the religious left, as I like to think of them, seeing as how they live their lives by a certain dogma, have now determined that poor people are terribly under-represented on America's college campuses. It was, I suppose, only a matter of time. After all, if no institute of higher education can justify its existence unless its student population is composed of X percent of women, Hispanics, blacks, gays, and the physically handicapped, some Democrat was bound to notice that there still remained an untapped source of future votes — namely, poor, young whites.

Diversity in the student body is the catch phrase. But, as you may have noticed, there is no parallel diversity along the faculties. In the humanities departments of most American colleges, professors run the gamut from liberal to radical. Given a choice between Castro and Bush, a large majority would vote for the Cuban dictator.

Frankly, I see no reason to give preferential treatment to students for no better reason than that their parents are poor. If a mix of humanity is what they're really seeking, I say they should throw open the doors to idiots. And, no, I'm not referring to those afore-mentioned profs who get paid a lot of money for doing nothing more than foisting their half-baked politics on a bunch of highly-impressionable eighteen-year-olds. No, I'm talking about the gen-uine article — people with subterranean I.Q.s.

I mean, if diversity is of such monumental importance, why limit it to race, gender and national origin? Obviously, members of these groups have far more in common with each other than they have with the intellectually-challenged — or whatever it is that the P.C. crowd is calling dumb people this week.

Honestly, I haven't a clue why college would be a more exalting experience just because the student in the next seat has different pigmentation or hails from a country where indoor plumbing is optional.

Admittedly, it's been many years since I was a collegian. Still, as I recall, the real value of the four years, aside from learning how to drink and how to talk to women without stuttering, was the enforced proximity to the minds and works of Socrates, Newton, Freud, Shakespeare, Plato, Milton, Michelangelo, Einstein, Da Vinci, and Jefferson, and was neither enhanced nor diminished by the color or creed of the other students.

The truth of the matter was that my interest in my fellow schol-ars, and I don't think my attitude was at all atypical, was limited to wanting to date the more attractive coeds and wanting to murder those brainiacs most likely to raise the class curve.

Inasmuch as smart, poor kids already receive academic scholar-ships, one can only assume that it's the stupid ones whom the social engineers are trying to cram through the ivied portals. But, inas-much as once in, they're destined to flunk out, I have a better solu-tion. I suggest we take our lead from *The Wizard of Oz*. The Scarecrow, as you may recall, didn't waste four years boning up for final exams. The great and powerful Oz merely handed him a diploma, and just like that, Ray Bolger was squaring the hypotenuse and jabbering away like William F. Buckley, Jr.

Why not give diplomas to anybody who wants one? In a day and age when people are wasting their parents' hard-earned money majoring in things like gay studies, sitcoms of the '60s, and comic books as literature, why not do the decent thing and just hand out sheepskins to anyone who says, "Please?" A built-in bonus of my plan is that with all those goobers off the campuses, there would be additional parking spaces for the people studying to be doctors, architects, and scientists.

After all, when all is said and done, college graduates aren't really smarter than other people. They just think they are.

• 66 •

Putting Tenure on Trial

An ongoing problem I have is that I am, at heart, a crusader, but, by temperament, a couch potato. To be really good at altering the status quo, you have to be ready to join with others in a mission, and I don't happen to like group activities. Even when a group consists of people I like as individuals, as soon as they organize, some bossy person is handing out marching orders, and somebody else is putting me to sleep reading the minutes of the last meeting.

Ideally, the way it should work is that I come up with great ideas and then get to lie down on the sofa and take a nap while other people run off and do the heavy lifting.

My latest campaign is to do away with tenure. If there's a dumber idea floating around than the guarantee of lifetime employment I'm not sure I want to hear about it. A person can take only so much stupidity in a single lifetime, and I believe I've just about reached my quota.

So far as I'm aware, the only two groups that receive tenure in our society are Supreme Court justices and teachers. The theory is that these people need to be protected from undue political pressure. Well, these days, as we're all very much aware, there is as much or more blatant politicking involved in a Supreme Court appointment than in a presidential election. For the life of me, I don't see why a duly elected president can only serve eight years, but a justice can serve thirty or forty.

It makes even less sense that professors are guaranteed a job for life. Guys on the assembly line don't have tenure. Gardeners and waitresses don't get tenure. Why should professors who already work short hours for good money be treated like English royalty?

I have heard the argument that, without such guarantees, they might be fired for political reasons. The fact of the matter is that, as more and more colleges and universities are infested with left wing radicals, professors are far more likely to be hired because of their politics.

As for the risk that a professor of any political stripe might be shown the exit because the administration disapproves of his leanings, the question should be moot. Even if his field of study happens to be history, philosophy or even the Republican party in the 21st century, no professor worth his salt has any business dragging his own politics into the classroom. But suggest that to a left wing academic and he starts yelling about censorship, as if the job description includes proselytizing.

To paraphrase George Bernard Shaw: those who can, teach; those who can't, indoctrinate.

Instead of tenure, I'd give these academics with their childish Che Guevara posters the gate.

• 67 •

A Word to the Wise and the Not So Wise

I'm here to announce that we are not a nation of scholars. Good lord, we're barely literate. It's a wonder that more of us don't walk around with our knuckles dragging on the ground. And it's about time that high school counselors and all the rest of us quit pretending that every seventeen- and eighteen-year-old squirt should be shoehorned into college and university.

Probably half, maybe three-quarters of the kids wandering around the groves of academe have no legitimate reason to be there. Of course I realize that in order for those youngsters to be out in the work force where they belong, employers have to stop demanding a B.A. as a prerequisite to employment. Most jobs just aren't all that demanding.

Like youth, a liberal arts education is generally wasted on the young. If the kids aren't majoring in engineering, medicine or math, they're probably just goofing off. There's nothing wrong with goofing off. That's how most grownups spend their weekends. Hard-working, well-meaning parents, however, should not be mortgaging their futures so that their sprouts can devote four years to avoiding the job market.

Obviously some people are luckier than others when it comes to finding their true vocations. If, for instance, you're born a Fonda, Barrymore, or Carradine, it would appear you get a SAG card along with your birth certificate. If you're named Rockefeller, you're not only born with a silver spoon in your mouth, you also have a knife, a fork, and a finger bowl in there. And if your name happens to be Kennedy, even before you learn to crawl it seems you're running for office.

If you're born into certain families, you're almost certain to wind up a classical musician. If you're born into others, you're just as likely to wind up in the linen, cement, and/or olive oil business, and on a first-name basis with several members of the U.S. Justice Department.

While I'm handing out good, sound advice, I'll suggest Michael Moore would be wise to quit making his so-called documentaries. I understand he is currently at work on one dealing with HMOs. Frankly, I'd like to see someone lower the boom on those outfits. Someone, but not Michael Moore. He has earned such a reputation for cinematic sins of commission and omission that any movie bearing his name is immediately suspect.

If Moore insists on pursuing a movie career, he should start cranking out flicks that don't pretend to be factual. Better yet, he should set his camera aside and run for public office. Unlike documentary filmmakers, politicians are expected to fib and fabricate. It's in the job description.

My last piece of advice is directed to all those highly impressionable teenagers taking up space on college campuses. Every time I see kids like you, full of hubris and attitude, giving standing ovations to the likes of Indian wannabe Ward Churchill, I get a stomachache.

I know you're young, and I know you're dumb, but even so, there's a limit to how much slack you should expect. I mean, it's not your fault that you're not as cute and as adorable as you were when you were four or five, but there's really no excuse for not being any brighter after all this time.

Let me suggest that aging hippies deserve to be ridiculed, not revered. Just because some long-haired galoot tells you he's smarter than your folks doesn't make it so. If he tells you that *you're* smarter than your folks, he's definitely lying to you and, what's worse, pandering to your worst instincts.

Keep in mind, children, that true revolutionaries are not pulling down $100,000 a year as tenured academics, no matter how badly they dress, no matter how long they wear their hair, and no matter how long they go between baths.

And, finally, one last word: Che Guevara was a schmuck!

Chapter Thirteen

A PARTY THAT INCLUDES
TED KENNEDY, HILLARY CLINTON,
AL GORE, JOHN KERRY, ROBERT BYRD,
MICHAEL MOORE, HOWARD DEAN,
AL FRANKEN, GEORGE SOROS,
AND JIMMY CARTER
IS MY IDEA OF A WAKE

• 68 •

Conservatives are from Mars, Liberals are from San Francisco

I don't know about the rest of you, but I have been finding it harder and harder to avoid thinking badly about liberals. I keep having to remind myself that I know any number of them that I like personally — including a couple of U.S. congressmen I've been friends with since college days — but, more and more often, I find I have to limit conversational topics to movies, baseball, and the weather lest their lack of logic and common sense incite me to riot.

I happen to live in California — arguably the most liberal state in the Union — a state in which the likes of Barbara Boxer, Dianne Feinstein, Jerry Brown, and Nancy Pelosi, all hold high elective office, and Ed Asner, Martin Sheen, Julia Roberts, Rob Reiner, Alec Baldwin, Barbra Streisand, and Susan Sarandon seem to think they do. I'm not asking for your pity, though I surely deserve it. I merely mention my home state because it has provided me with such a perfect laboratory in which to study lefties in their natural habitat.

What first comes to mind isn't even their tedious cant, it's their hypocrisy. They will lecture one and all about global warming. They will disrupt the building of homes and offices, lest a species of snail be displaced. They will nest for months in some tree that a developer — the man who owns the tree — wishes to cut down or even move to a different location. They will conduct candlelight vigils if anyone even mentions the possibility of oil drilling in Alaska.

However, nowhere on earth will you find more gas-guzzling SUVs on the road. The Hummers in Beverly Hills alone, are enough to make an Army tank commander salivate with envy.

In matters ecological, as in all else, it's always a case with liberals of do as I say, not as I do. You may have noticed that those on the far left have pictured George W. Bush as the Anti-Christ when it comes to ecology because he favors drilling for oil in the Yukon, but they never had a cross word for Saddam Hussein, even though his burning of the Kuwaiti oil fields ranks among the very worst ecological disasters in history.

Liberals are forever bemoaning the plight of the downtrodden, always eager to play the class card or the race card. However, as often as not, they're the ones who own the sweat shops and restaurants where the Hispanics toil for minimum wage. It's in their pricey homes where cleaning ladies and nannies from Guatemala and Honduras mop, vacuum, and raise the children while being paid under the table. Liberals are all for higher minimum wages and a thriving Social Security, just so long as it doesn't cost them an extra dime.

At the drop of a hat, liberals will deliver a speech on the glories of democracy. However, out here, when the citizens overwhelmingly vote for capital punishment or against subsidizing illegal aliens, liberals can always be counted on to rustle up an appeals judge eager to nullify the will of the people.

And isn't it strange that although it's those on the left who constantly claim they're the ones looking out for the poor, the oppressed, the disenfranchised, I've often heard liberals dismiss 250 million of their fellow Americans as "those people we fly over" when going from L.A. to New York. I swear I've never heard a similar remark from a conservative.

Recently, I received an e-mail from a man I didn't know, in response to a piece I'd written lauding President Bush. Not satisfied with merely attacking me as a know-nothing, he proceeded to argue that Bush had only won the election in 2000 because he carried "so many rural states." Clearly, in his universe, only urbanites are real Americans. So, while liberals will sing folk songs celebrating the wonderful folks who build the bridges, till the soil and run the railroads, they just don't want them voting.

Liberals pat themselves on the back for being the only truly colorblind people in society. Yet they're the ones crusading for Affirmative Action, insisting that certain segments be allowed to leapfrog over the harder-working and better-qualified students for no other reason than their color.

Liberals always boast that theirs is the party of inclusion, proudly boasting that they're home to the likes of Maxine Waters, Al Sharpton and Jesse Jackson — three people most of us wouldn't even want to have over for dinner. Waters is the woman, after all, who not only argued for Ebonics being taught in the inner-city schools, but insisted that crack cocaine was a conspiracy concocted by the CIA to undermine the black community; and this was long after the newspaper that had published the "scoop" came clean, admitting they'd been taken in by a hoax!

Sharpton is the weasel who rode to media prominence by claiming a black girl had been raped by New York cops. He never recanted, even after the girl confessed she had trumped up the story after spending a weekend shacked up with her teenage boyfriend, to avoid being disciplined by her mother!

Jesse Jackson started out lying about Martin Luther King's dying in his arms and went on to distinguish himself by calling New York "Hymietown," siring an illegitimate child, raising corporate extortion to an art form, and cavorting with any dictator who'd make a hefty donation to his Rainbow Coalition.

On the other hand, when you hear liberals badmouthing the likes of Clarance Thomas, Colin Powell, Thomas Sowell, Miguel

Estrada, Walter Williams, Larry Elder, Ward Connerly and Condoleezza Rice, you'd think you were listening to old Herman Talmadge laying into some poor black sharecropper. No matter how distinguished a member of a minority group may be, if he or she doesn't toe the party line, the hounds of the left can be counted on to start barking, "Oreo," "Uncle Tom," and "sell out."

For me, there's nothing like hearing a political hack like Ted Kennedy insisting that some honorable American isn't "black enough" or "Hispanic enough" to pass muster. Isn't it the least bit odd that Kennedy's been allowed to hold down a job in the federal government for all these years even though one could have said with some justification that the Chappaquiddick Kid was never "smart enough" or "decent enough" or even "sober enough" to be a United States senator?

Liberals speak out against special interest groups every chance they get, except of course their own. Exorbitant medical insurance fees, caused by outrageous jury awards, is driving doctors and surgeons out of business and leaving the state of health care a shambles. However, trial lawyers are making billions and funneling off a lot of it to the Democratic party. So, not a peep do we hear from the left side of the aisle.

Every objective study confirms that bilingual education is a rotten way to teach Spanish-speaking kids. At an age when mastering a new language is a snap, these children are weaned so slowly off their native tongue that many of them never catch up academically. But the teachers union, more concerned with its coffers than the kids, pushes for a bilingual curriculum because it successfully lobbied for a measure that pays bilingual teachers a 10% bonus. They, in turn, tithe the Democratic party.

Unlike trial lawyers, whom we all know to be immoral parasites, abettors to rapists and pedophiles, one would hope that teachers would be ashamed to sacrifice their charges for a handful of silver.

But liberals prove over and over again that they are shameless. Just how hypocritical are those on the left? Well, Sen. Dianne Feinstein, who's made a career out of fighting against a private, law-abiding citizen owning a gun, was discovered to be a pistol-packing mama. The Hollywood crowd made a big deal out of turning in some of their artillery, but you may have noticed that none of their bodyguards ever disarmed.

Actor Alan Alda used to give rousing speeches at NOW conventions and receive standing ovations for telling the ladies how he and his wife were equal partners. But for the first eight or nine seasons of "M*A*S*H," no woman wrote or directed an episode unless it was one featuring "Hot Lips," in which case Loretta Swit would insist on it. Yet nobody at NOW ever asked Alda, who pretty much ran the show after the first couple of years, why women weren't given a fair crack. But, then, liberals never put other liberals on the hot seat.

Norman Lear also got a standing ovation from NOW delegates when he announced that he was donating $250,000 to the organization in the name of Edith Bunker. At the time, he had two vice presidents in his company, two people who allegedly had equal power and authority. What wasn't equal was their salary. The man was paid $125,000 a year; the woman, $75,000. So we have Lear, a wealthy contributor to liberal causes and election campaigns, giving away a quarter of a million dollars in the name of a fictional female character while underpaying a female employee to the tune of fifty grand a year. For what it's worth, he was also known to underpay his female office staff.

But the list goes on and on. Liberals complain that the rich get more money back than the poor when there's a tax cut, ignoring the obvious fact that if you pay more in, it makes sense that you would get more back. I have even heard some of them bemoaning the fact that the very poor wouldn't get any money back, even while I know acknowledging that low income earners don't even pay federal income tax! One can't help wondering in what bizarro universe these people dwell.

These are the same folks who insist that the French and the Russians were guided by matters of conscience when they objected to war with Iraq, while Bush's agenda was driven by oil madness. How dedicated to ignoring the truth do people have to be to overlook the fact it that was Russia and France that had the billion dollar oil deals with Saddam Hussein?

It's the same people who saw no reason for Clinton to deal with Congress or the U.N. when he invaded Somalia, bombed Sudan, and sent troops to Kosovo, who saw no inconsistency in demanding that Bush had to get approval from everyone, including the baseball commissioner and his third grade teacher, before blowing his nose.

Their juvenile placards and slogans insisted that Bush was rushing to war. We all know that he was anything but rash, but once liberals glom onto a line that like, they will repeat it, parrot-like, parading with their "No Blood for Oil" and "Bush = Hitler" placards until the cows come home.

Liberals, often under the banner of the ACLU, will lead the charge for religious freedom. But when you check the record, you find that the religious practices they defend tend to be those that involve the smoking of marijuana, the ingesting of peyote buttons, and the ritualistic slaughtering of small animals. Where they draw the line is when it come to the barbaric practices of hanging Christmas wreaths and lighting menorahs.

Liberals insist they love the Constitution, but they hate the Second Amendment like poison. They insist they love America, but they abhor patriotism. They point to Europe as the role model to which we should aspire, but they never move there. And invariably they fail to acknowledge that, for some crazy reason, people seeking freedom and liberty always seem to be headed in our direction and never away.

They tell us, when Clinton gets in hot water because of his sexual peccadilloes and his proclivity for perjury, that we should be as sophisticated as the French, and be above such things. They seem to forget that when the much-hated Richard Nixon was driven out of office, it was the very same French who couldn't understand what we were getting so excited about. Ah, the French, so continental, so sophisticated, so full of shit. It is my suggestion that the next time Germany or Switzerland or Luxembourg or even little, tiny Monaco decides to invade France, we let them.

When Elia Kazan received his honorary academy award a few years back, liberals marched around the auditorium carrying signs denouncing the director for having named names fifty years earlier. When he came on stage, instead of the usual standing ovation, he garnered slight applause and the TV cameras focused on Nick Nolte, Amy Madigan, and Ed Harris sitting on their hands and glowering at the feeble old man. Keep in mind that Hollywood is a town built on betrayal and backstabbing. Kazan's sin was not in ratting out his old friends, but in ratting out his old Communist friends. If his old pals had been Nazis or fascists, they'd have erected a statue in his honor at Hollywood and Vine.

Not too long ago, a blacklisted writer, John Sanford, died at the age of ninety. To his dying day, he remained a member of the Communist Party. One of his friends, quoted in a fulsome tribute printed in the *Los Angeles Times,* said that Sanford's political convictions were set in the 1930s and never wavered. That was intended as a compliment. Imagine a man whose politics were set so deep in concrete that through seven decades of Stalin, the Hitler pact, the atomic spy trials, the massacres in Cambodia and Hungary, the enslavement of Eastern Europe, Khrushchev's speech to the Soviet

Congress, etc., etc., etc., the man never entertained a single doubt that what he believed in his 20s was gospel. Priests have doubts. Nuns have doubts. Nuclear physicists have doubts. I suspect that even God has doubts. Only liberals are immune.

It was once observed, and with good reason, that a man who isn't a liberal at 20 has no heart, and that a man who isn't a conservative at 40 has no brain.

Most of the conservatives I know, including myself, started out somewhere else on the political spectrum, and evolved through time and knowledge and experience. I personally do not know of a single case of an individual evolving in the other direction. I will leave it to the Darwinists to make of that what they will.

• 69 •
Voices from the Left

For years, I've hated listening to the infantile blathering of America's leftists. All that was required for me to come down with a splitting headache was to hear John Kerry, Robert Byrd, or Joseph Biden insist that if only they were running things, gas would cost 25 cents a gallon, peace would reign in the Middle East, and Ruth Bader Ginsburg would be the most conservative justice on the Supreme Court.

However, not too long ago, I had an epiphany. It's not just that the liberals are annoying because of what they say, but because of the way they say it. Have you listened to Al Gore lately? He's as loud as a pneumatic drill. And you would think that after his meltdown following the Iowa primary, Howard Dean would tone it down a notch. Instead, he's revved up the noise level until he sounds like a chimpanzee on speed.

But all of that is performance art. The moment these politicians see a live microphone or a TV camera, they simply can't control themselves. The poor creatures are like Pavlov's dogs salivating at the sound of a bell.

However, if there's anything worse than having to listen to these shnooks screaming to the choir, it's having to listen to the ladies on the left. I refer to the sisterhood that includes the likes of Susan Estrich, Teresa Heinz-Kerry, Nancy Pelosi, Gloria Allred, Barbara Boxer, Cindy Sheehan, Barbra Streisand and, of course, Hillary Clinton. Each and every one of them has a voice that sounds like fingernails raking a blackboard.

I don't want to suggest that their speaking voices are all alike, aside from the fact that each has the power to make your ears bleed. Some, after all, are whinier than others, some are harsher, while a few are so nasal you'd think that Estrich, for instance, must have adenoids the size of grapefruits.

And let us not forget Jane Fonda, the *grande dame* of the left. Even before she became the pin-up queen of the Viet Cong, it always amazed me that she was able to have an acting career in spite of being cursed with a voice that sounded like it had been transplanted from a screech owl.

It occurred to me one day that Fonda has a voice that every divorced man associates with his ex-wife, and reminds him all over again why he was so willing, even anxious, to divvy up the community property.

• 70 •
He's Not Heavy, He's My History Book

As you may have noticed, when liberals want to stereotype conservatives, they usually bring up creationists as if every religious person in America discounts Darwin and walks around with his knuckles dragging on the ground. In spite of having such obviously big brain types as Christopher and William Buckley, Dick Cheney, Walter Williams, John and Norman Podhoretz, Dennis Prager, Condoleezza Rice, Dick Rumsfeld, Robert Bork, Mark Levin, David Horowitz, Joseph Farah, Ann Coulter, Michelle Malkin, Antonin Scalia, Thomas Sowell, Charles Krauthammer, and Michael Medved on our side, the liberals much prefer to concentrate on simple, often ill-educated, but basically decent people who simply don't happen to share their values.

On the other hand, when conservatives take on liberals, they don't revile the undereducated blocs of voters that make up a major part of their party's constituency, but instead target the kingpins of the left — the likes of Boxer and Feinstein, Clinton and Schumer, Murray and Reid, Pelosi and Byrd, Kennedy and Kerry, Leahy and Dean, George Soros and Michael Moore — people who are richer than God and have all the college degrees money can buy.

To give you some idea how liberals, when they're in the majority, think, you merely have to consider California state assembly bill 756. Hold on to your hats because this one's a doozy. It bans school districts from purchasing history textbooks that are longer than 200 pages!

One of the sponsors of the bill, assemblywoman Jackie Goldberg, in arguing on its behalf, actually said, "The schools are teaching kids with the same kinds of massive books that were used generations ago, although the world has changed significantly."

Now if I follow what we'll laughingly refer to as her logic, although we have many years of additional history to deal with, the obvious solution is to make the books much shorter. Perhaps, if she had her way, Mrs. Goldberg would have *The New York Times* change its motto from All the News That's Fit to Print to All the News That Fits.

But why stop there? Why not cut every other word out of the Bible and every other page out of the dictionary? Ten Commandments? Why not five? Seven deadly sins? How about just two?

Let's face it, assembly bill 756 sounds like a totally goofy notion at first. But the more I think about it, the more sense it begins to make. After all, when you stop and realize how dumb Mrs. Goldberg and her liberal colleagues in Sacramento must be, would you want to risk having your kids and grandkids using the same learning materials they used?

• 71 •
Doing Away with the Poor

It is alleged that when his ex-wife was asked to sum up William Saroyan, famous for his heartwarming stories about Fresno's Armenian community, she replied, "Bill loved mankind, but he hated people."

Knowing from firsthand experience how bitter ex-wives can be, I can't comment on the veracity of that rather pithy analysis, but I think it's a very appropriate comment when it comes to large numbers of Democrats.

The specific group I have in mind includes several millionaire members of the U.S. Senate, virtually every major figure in the motion picture and popular music industries, and a slew of business tycoons. The one thing all these muckety mucks have in common is they only mingle with each other. They love mankind, but they hate poor people. That's why they live behind high walls and electric gates and travel everywhere in limos and private jets, generally accompanied by extremely large men carrying extremely large guns.

When it comes to speaking at charity banquets and delivering political speeches, the rich and famous will say all the usual compassionate bilge about the poor and the downtrodden. But so far as actually interacting with them, that's strictly limited to the peons who mop their floors, cook their food, mow their lawns, and look after their kids.

And, frankly, I don't blame them. I mean, who the heck really wants to hang around poor people? Besides not looking or even smelling as good as rich people, they always want something. And usually what they want more than anything is to be rich. That's exactly the sort of thing that makes wealthy people really nervous. After all, it's not their own kind who go around starting revolutions, burgling their homes, kidnapping for ransom, or knocking them on the head to steal their wallets.

So it is we have millionaires like Kennedy and Kerry, Edwards and Feinstein, Boxer and Dean, trying to pass themselves off as populists, yammering about raising taxes and soaking the rich as if they themselves were members in good standing of the lunch bucket brigade. The odd thing is that so many poor people seem so willing to go along with the gag. That can either be attributed to extremely good manners or a naïvete bordering on feeblemindedness.

In any case, being neither rich nor poor myself, perhaps it's no surprise that, being in a position to view the problem objectively, I have been able to come up with a surefire cure for poverty in America.

I'm not sure if it's this way in other parts of the country, but here in Southern California, individuals and companies get to adopt a mile or two of freeway. I'm not sure what their responsibility is, inasmuch as the orange-vested clean up crews consist, so far as I can tell, of bad drivers performing the community service portion of their sentences and not of Rosanne Barr or the gang at Morton's Mufflers. But I figure they must have kicked in a pretty penny in order to get their names on those little highway signs. After all, publicity doesn't come cheap in this town.

Well, it struck me that if the well-to-do are willing to adopt a stretch of the 405, why don't they, instead, adopt the poor? Heck, all by themselves, liberals like Ted Turner, Barbara Streisand, and George Soros can afford to adopt every illegal alien coming across the border. And what's more, Ben & Jerry's leftist ice cream moguls Ben Cohen and Jerry Greenfield can provide them with butter pecan and fudge ripple until the cows come home.

72

Full of Bluster

Probably because *Mr. Smith Goes to Washington* has always been one of my favorite movies — and was the movie for which Jimmy Stewart should have won his Oscar instead of the over-rated *Philadelphia Story* — I have always had a soft spot for filibusters.

When I was just a kid, a gadfly senator from Oregon named Wayne Morse appeared to be conducting one-man filibusters every other week. He was constantly holding the floor of the U.S. Senate, it seems, for 20 or 30 hours at a stretch. I always had a sneaky hunch that *Mr. Smith Goes to Washington* had been one of Senator Morse's favorite movies, too.

So it is that I have been particularly dismayed with the Democrats for ruining the darn things. It's not supposed to be a team sport, after all. If you've got 45 shmoes taking part, it's not a filibuster, it's a damn vaudeville act.

You can imagine how I felt when the Democrats, in a feeble attempt to defend their judicial obstructionism, made a TV commercial that showed us Jimmy Stewart in that marvelous scene where he lost his voice, but never his integrity. It so happens I knew Jimmy Stewart — a lifelong Republican, by the way — and believe me, Robert Byrd, Patrick Leahy, and Ted Kennedy are no Jimmy Stewart. And John Kerry is certainly no Jefferson Smith.

The Democrats actually have the gall to say that they're only opposing judges who are out of the mainstream. This coming from a bunch of left wingers who picked mad Howard Dean to head up their party, and selected radicals like Nancy Pelosi and Howard Reid to lead them in the House and Senate! These people are so far out of the mainstream, they'd need a compass and a team of Sherpas to find the shoreline and a dowser to find water.

The liberals in the U.S. Senate claim that they're merely carrying out their sworn duty by opposing presidential appointments with which they take issue. But the Constitution gives the power to appoint judges to the president, limiting the role of the Senate to advise and consent, not to veto.

Then, for good measure, the Democrats insist that such appointments should require not simple majorities of 51 votes in the Senate, but supermajorities of 60! Again, there is no constitutional basis for such a requirement. The Constitution is very specific when it comes to these matters. Supermajorities are required when treaties are involved or when it comes to amending the Constitution, but not when it comes to placing judges on the bench.

Finally, the Democrats are claiming that the Republicans are trying to run roughshod over them. What they understandably choose to ignore is that in a democracy, when one party controls the White House and has sizeable majorities in both houses of Congress, it's the people that have run roughshod over them. And under those circumstances, a filibuster is not democracy in action; it's sheer demagoguery.

In fact, it is because the Democrats cannot win elections that they are so desperate to make certain that only like-minded judges are appointed. As you may have noticed, the only way they have to promote their left wing agenda is through activist judges who, by ignoring the constitutional limits of their office, legislate from the bench.

Because ours is a representative government, the 45 Democrats in the Senate are fully entitled to have their say. What they are not entitled to have is the final say.

• 73 •

In This Corner, Wearing Brass Knuckles, Susan Estrich

Out here, in L.A., we have recently been treated to a colossal hissy fit that had liberals gunning for other liberals. One would think that any right-thinking conservative would happily sit back and watch the blood run in the gutters. But even in a battle royal that pits left-ies against their own kind, a fair-minded person can't help taking sides.

On one side, you have the knee-jerk liberal editors at the *L.A. Times* wearing the white trunks or, in this case, at least the white hats; on the other side, you have the idly rich women of the Westside — most of them the wives or ex-wives of multi-million-aires like Michael Huffington, Bud Yorkin and Larry David. They're the sort of ladies who, because they might have undocumented maids, nannies, and gardeners from Mexico and Guatemala working for them, not only favor open borders but believe they're in line for canonization. These are the knuckleheads who support NOW and the ACLU and who yammer about fossil fuels and the ozone layer while they gad about in SUVs and private jets.

Perhaps not as wealthy as some of her cohorts, but equally self-deluded is Susan Estrich. Today, she's a law professor at USC; in the past, she was the campaign manager for Michael Dukakis. Somehow, Ms. Estrich has turned an annoyingly nasal voice, a painted-on smirk, and a ton of attitude into a secondary career as one of TV's talking heads.

Recently, she declared a jihad against the *Times* because she had decided that they don't publish nearly enough female columnists. She even had the chutzpah to assign her college students to keeping track. Apparently — assuming that her law students are able to count — the *Times* was publishing men four times as often as they were publishing women. And, most tellingly, they weren't publishing Ms. Estrich at all!

The editors, fools that they are, took the charge to heart. In their lame defense, they countered the accusation by pointing out that they published women more frequently than did such liberal citadels as *The New York Times* and the *Washington Post*. Ms. Estrich and her cohorts replied that what other papers do or don't do is no defense for what the *Times* does or doesn't do.

Then, when she realized that the *Times* wasn't about to knuckle under to the ladies who lunch, she stooped to suggesting that perhaps editor Michael Kinsley's brain had been adversely affected by his illness. The man suffers from Parkinson's.

At one fell swoop, Estrich not only struck a new low in debating tactics, but by trying to score points off the man's illness, proved that in her case at least it's compassionate *liberal* that's the oxymoron.

The fact is, if anybody should be complaining about being underrepresented on the paper's op-ed page, it's not women, it's conservatives. By way of tokenism, once a week they run something by Max Boot. The rest of the week, they run letters to the editor from readers berating Boot.

If women get to sound off 20% of the time in the *Times,* I'd say that's roughly ten times as much space as writers from the right receive. Of course I'm only guessing. Unlike Professor Estrich, I don't have a cadre of eager coeds to do my counting for me.

The worst thing about Estrich and the other members of her overly pampered platoon is that they're hypocrites. It's not really female writers they want to see in the *Times,* it's female left wing writers. I guarantee if Ann Coulter, Tammy Bruce, and Michelle Malkin started showing up on a regular basis, these wealthy, self-important, elitists would be descending on the *Times* armed with tar and feathers.

The truth is, with this gaggle of geese, agenda always trumps gender.

• 74 •
If Only Clinton Had Been a Republican

The way that so many people, especially politicians, went nuts over the ports deal reminded me once again what a difference party designation makes. One only has to compare how harshly Sam Alito was treated during his confirmation hearings with the way that the ACLU's chief counsel, Ruth Bader Ginsberg, sailed through hers.

Getting back to the matter of the ports, I'm still not sure if it was a good idea or a bad one to allow the United Arab Emirates to manage those installations on the East Coast. But I'm awfully curious why some of those same people who wanted Bush's head on a pike weren't the least bit upset when, during Clinton's reign, Communist China was granted the authority to manage ports on the West Coast. So far as I'm concerned, anybody who believes we have more to fear from Dubai than from Beijing needs a brain transplant.

It was only after Saddam Hussein bought off several nations with his oil-for-food scam and ignored a kazillion U.N. resolutions that Bush invaded Iraq. Immediately, the cry went up that he didn't have a coalition. Afterwards, the complaint was that he lacked an exit strategy. Odd that nobody said "boo" when Clinton unilaterally invaded Somalia; odder still that when he sent troops to Kosovo, promising they'd be home within a year, nobody took him to task when, a few years later, when he left the Oval Office, our forces were still there. That's some exit strategy.

His liberal critics accuse Bush of being in bed with Halliburton, but Halliburton, you should be aware, did just fine in the 90s when Clinton was minding the store.

You also hear about Bush pandering to Enron. Well, there's no denying that the sleazebags at Enron donated over $400,000 to the party and kicked in another $100,000 to help pay for the president's inauguration. And there's no getting around the fact that Enron's chairman stayed at the White House on 11 different occasions. Talk about having access! What's more, the Export-Import Bank subsidized Enron to the tune of $600 million in a single transaction.

Clearly, where Enron is concerned, the president has a lot to answer for. But the president we're talking about happens to be Clinton. Bush, in case you didn't notice, is the president whose administration brought Enron CEO Ken Lay up on charges.

Clinton is the same fellow who had Yasser Arafat as a house guest seemingly every other week, while Bush is the guy who declared the terrorist persona non grata.

His enemies like to charge Bush with being in league with the Saudis, but at least the sheiks provide us with oil. Nary a peep was heard, however, when Clinton handed over military technology to the Red Chinese in exchange for nothing more than campaign contributions.

There's one last thing about Clinton. We keep hearing that he was the first black president. Aside from the fact that he and that other serial adulterer, Jesse Jackson, allegedly prayed together when they were both caught tom-catting around, what made Clinton so darn black? Heck, taking his lead from Congress, he even revamped welfare and tried to get recipients weaned off the federal teat. If Clinton had been a Republican, the Black Caucus would have stormed the White House with torches and pitchforks.

Aside from Jackson, the only black person Clinton seemed to hang around with was Vernon Jordan. I spent eight years trying to figure out what he did for a living. I finally narrowed it down to two things. He had to let Clinton beat him at golf, and when things got too hot with Monica Lewinsky, it was Jordan's responsibility to get her out of town and try to find her a job in New York City.

But I never was able to get a handle on what made Clinton blacker than, say, George W. Bush. It's Bush, after all, who has appointed Colin Powell and Condi Rice to the highest positions in his cabinet. You would think that would count for something with the left, especially with one of them being a woman.

So what made Clinton so black? That he spoke with a southern accent, played a musical instrument, came from a dysfunctional family, and was blatantly promiscuous?

If that sounds racist, don't blame me. I never regarded Clinton as a credit to any race — black, white, or human.

• 75 •
Are Liberals Really Lemmings?

It can't be easy being a liberal these days. For one thing, in a desperate attempt to make inroads with the electorate, they not only can't speak like liberals, but outside a few blue spots on the American map, they don't even dare identify themselves as such. Instead, they've begun calling themselves progressives. Frankly, it sounds like a Madison Avenue brainstorm. But instead of coming up with a whole new name, they might as well have simply advertised themselves as liberals, but New and Improved!

As a result of this approach, you have Nancy Pelosi, left-winger from San Francisco, trying to pass herself off as the second Mother Teresa, except for the part about washing the feet of lepers. With her newfound religiosity, don't be surprised if she starts talking in tongues, although, come to think of it, that wouldn't be much worse than the way she usually sounds.

Then we have Hillary Clinton's posing as a centrist. I suppose she is one, if centrist is someone whose politics place her right in between John Kerry and Ted Kennedy. Otherwise, her best chance of fooling anyone is by donning a Harry Truman mask this Halloween.

Whether they call themselves liberals, progressives or Whigs, the Democrats never change their modus operandi. They continue waging class and race warfare while simultaneously condemning the Republicans for being divisive. Led by Howard Dean, the mad munchkin, the party continues to shake campaign contributions out of the usual suspects — trial lawyers, deep-pocket unions, George Soros, and the Hollywood fruitcakes.

When you see the sleazy levels to which the liberals will stoop, the big mystery to me is how the Democrats manage to do better in general elections than the Libertarians or the Vegetarians, for that matter. It's not just that they continue trying to gain suffrage for illegal aliens and even criminals behind bars simply because they know that a resounding majority in both groups will vote for them, either. For instance, a recent study by the nonpartisan ACVR Legislative Fund disclosed what many of us suspected; namely, that it was the Democrats, not the Republicans, who pulled off virtually all of the dirty tricks during the 2004 election. Especially in such places as Milwaukee, Seattle, Philadelphia, St. Louis, and Cleveland, liberal thugs slashed the tires of GOP election day vans; phoned Republicans, giving them the wrong date for the election and the wrong location of their polling places; intimidated elderly voters and even assaulted some. In short, they were doing the very things they were accusing the Republicans of doing. And the major media, being the major media, saw to it that their lies were repeated and never questioned.

The Democrats claim they want Bush to nominate moderate, middle-of-the-road judges. These are the same folks who, under Bill Clinton's stewardship, placed the former head counsel for the ACLU, Ruth Bader Ginsburg, on the Supreme Court. That should give you some idea of what they regard as moderate.

These are the same jackals who tore Judge Pickering to pieces, condemning him as a racist — a white Southerner who had stood up to the KKK, earning the love and respect of blacks in his own state — simply because the likes of Kennedy, Leahy, and Reid couldn't tolerate the idea of a conservative being in line to join Mrs. Ginsburg on the Court.

Now, as they gear up to trash Judge John Roberts, they're hoping to find that there was something unsavory about the way that the judge and his wife adopted their twins. If Joseph Welch were still alive, I'd like to think he'd look at the leadership of the Democratic party and say, as he once said to Sen. Joe McCarthy, "Finally, have you no shame?"

It's been about 140 years since the War Between the States ended. There is, I submit, a similar war being waged today. One could only wish that the opposition forces were being led by someone one-tenth as decent and honorable as Robert E. Lee.

Regrettably, that's not the case. As a result, we find ourselves in the midst of a battle royal whose outcome is every bit as important to America's future as was the Civil War. Thanks to the tactics and conduct of the Democrats, the current conflict might best be called the Uncivil War.

• 76 •
Judging the Judges

A question that bears looking into is whether a career in politics inevitably turns people into four-flushers or whether four-flushers are born, not made, and are simply drawn to the field the way that metal shavings are drawn to a magnet.

Being a conservative, naturally I hold Democrats in far lower regard than I do Republicans. But, overall, I don't think that politicians of any stripe should be trusted anywhere near a live microphone or anybody's wallet. In fact, I find most people's infatuation with office holders completely infantile and unseemly, and on a par with an adolescent girl's crush on some slack-jawed rock star.

After all, what does a pol do that is so admirable? He spends most of his waking hours shaking down friends and strangers for campaign funds so that he can remain in office…and continue shaking down friends and strangers for campaign funds.

In those odd moments when he takes a break from lining his own coffers, his work consists in coming up with novel and foolish ways to spend our tax dollars. And, stoopnagels that we are, we applaud him as if he'd just written a personal check!

Up to now, I've merely been generalizing about politicians as a group. But, for sheer unadulterated duplicity, you can't beat the left-wing members of the U.S. Senate, and don't even think about trying. You'd only hurt yourself.

As loathsome as they are on any given day, they rise to truly unimaginable heights on those occasions when they're sitting in judgment of a prospective jurist. Consider, for instance, the back alley mugging they administered to Judge Charles Pickering, a man who had faced down the Ku Klux Klan, condemning him as a racist, of all things, thus ensuring that this gallant gentleman would never be allowed to sit on the bench beside Ruth Bader Ginsburg. Well, perhaps there was an upside, after all, for Judge Pickering.

One only has to look at the way they attacked Sam Alito, by all accounts a decent man in both his public and private life, to realize the depths to which these moral pygmies will stoop in order to promote their leftist agenda. I find myself wondering how such fellows as Joseph Biden and Ted Kennedy would deal with judicial nominees carting around their own respective baggage.

Can't you just imagine the blood-letting that would occur if President Bush dared nominate a judge who, like Senator Biden, had seen his presidential hopes dashed when it was discovered that he had plagiarized another man's speech. Or imagine if the president had the gall to nominate somebody like Robert Byrd, the moral conscience of the Democratic party and a former member of the Ku Klux Klan.

Better yet, can't you picture the grilling that Kennedy, the swizzle stick kid himself, would give a candidate who had earned a well-deserved reputation as a college cheat, a sot, and a womanizer?

Finally, can't you envision the senior senator from Massachusetts leaning forward in his chair, peering down at the judicial wannabe over those glasses he always wears to such events, and saying in that overbearing voice that can curdle milk: "How dare you even think about sitting on the highest court in the land? Who are you to sit in judgment of any man? Does the name Mary Jo Kopechne not ring any bells for you? It surely does for me, sir. It surely does for me."

• 77 •

McKinney Rhymes with Ninny

As I sit here, I don't yet know if Rep. Cynthia McKinney is going to face criminal charges for hitting the officer. And, frankly, I'm not sure if I want to see her charged. It's not that I wouldn't be delighted at the prospect of having her marched off to the cooler. But the truth is that's not going to happen. Even if she were to be indicted, and even if they were to go to the trouble and expense of putting her on trial, are any of us so naïve as to expect a member of Congress — especially a female, and a black one at that — to do jail time?

Another reason I don't want them to go through the motions is that I have already seen enough of Rep. McKinney and heard enough from her to last me several lifetimes.

And still one more reason is that I don't want to find myself generalizing about the good people of Georgia, as I'm sure I would if I kept seeing this arrogant dimwit on the news night after night. After all, I live in Southern California, home of people like Barbra Streisand, Rob Reiner, and Charlie Sheen. So you can see why, living in this glass house, I'd prefer not to be tempted to throw stones. But, holy moly, you folks in Atlanta, who have elected this national embarrassment on six separate occasions, really do have some explaining to do.

The best excuse I can come up with is that by keeping her in Washington, you have managed to foist her off on the rest of us and kept her away from Peach Street.

But, when it comes to offending large groups of people, even

McKinney was no match for those mobs of Latinos who recently marched down the streets of America, waving Mexican flags. If that was someone's idea of the best way to win friends and influence people, that someone is an idiot.

Recently, I heard two guys on a sports show discussing the new pitching coach for the Atlanta Braves. They agreed he was well-qualified, but they felt he would be working under somewhat of a handicap because he didn't speak Spanish and would therefore have a problem communicating with certain members of the staff. No doubt they're right, but what I'd like to know is why these pitchers haven't taken the time to learn English. After all, it's no secret that from an early age, kids all over Latin America set their sights on playing ball in los Estados Unidos. We also know that certain American teams have created and subsidized baseball academies south of the border. So, how is it that nobody has taken the time to teach these kids something besides how to throw a slider and how to steal second when a southpaw's on the mound?

I probably shouldn't be too hard on the kids. After all, Rep. McKinney was born here, and she doesn't speak all that well.

But her basic message still comes through loud and clear. Namely, that nobody is to be allowed to take any black person to task for anything without being automatically accused of racism. People like Ms. McKinney, Harry Belafonte, Al Sharpton, Jesse Jackson, Charles Rangel, and Danny Glover remind me of riverboat gamblers. But instead of palming aces and dealing seconds, it's always the race card they've got tucked up their sleeve.

The whole sorry bunch of them are like the boy who cried "Wolf!" once too often. If an actual racist came anywhere near the sheep, nobody would believe these race hustlers.

In conclusion, I know that much has been made of the fact that perhaps the reason the officer didn't recognize Rep. McKinney was because she had recently changed her hairdo. My own theory is that he mistook her for someone else, and that when he tapped her on the shoulder it was only to ask for Buckwheat's autograph.

• 78 •
The Descent of Liberals

For the longest time, I thought that the main difference between those on the Left and those on the Right was that whereas conservatives believed that liberals were wrong on the issues, liberals were convinced that conservatives were just plain evil.

I still believe that to be the case, but I've also become aware that, in addition, leftists regard those on the other side as stupid. My basis for that is that they like nothing better than to stereotype us all as creationists while they wrap themselves up all snuggly and warm in Charles Darwin's theory of evolution.

Just to get all my cards on the table, I am not religious. I don't take either Testament as gospel. But that doesn't mean I think that those who do are ignorant or even a lower form of animal life. By and large, I think that religious people — yes, even born-again Christians and creationists — are often better people than those who aren't. By better, I mean more kindly, more decent, better friends, better neighbors, better parents.

So many people who know even less about science than I do, and who have never bothered reading any of Darwin's works, base their defense of his theory on Stanley Kramer's truly awful movie about the Scopes trial, *Inherit the Wind*.

Representing enlightenment, as Clarence Darrow, Kramer cast Hollywood's avuncular Spencer Tracy. As William Jennings Bryan, he mis-cast Fredric March, and then had him sweat and spray spittle for two solid hours. It was, by the way, the only time that the two fine actors, who had each starred in a version of *Dr. Jekyll and Mr.*

Hyde, worked together. With the notoriously heavy-handed Kramer at the helm, Tracy naturally came off like Jekyll, while March came off as Hyde.

It's true that Bryan was a loquacious fellow who'd never use one word when there were thirty or forty lying around just going to waste. Darrow, however, was the criminal defense attorney who, for an enormous fee, used his verbal skills to make certain that the vile Leopold and Loeb didn't die for the cold-blooded murder of young Bobby Franks. Between those two, I'd take my chances with Bryan. Better a bore than a man with innocent blood on his hands.

The fact of the matter is that it doesn't make much difference if Darwin was right or wrong. Really, how would it affect your life if his beliefs could be proven one way or the other? Unless you're one of the very small number of academics involved in evolutionary biology, it wouldn't make a scintilla of difference in your daily life. Even Darwin couldn't explain how everything began in the first place; his theories only dealt with the manner in which things evolved from some unexplainable point of origin. So if creationists choose to believe that God set everything in motion, and that belief makes them happy, there's nothing in Darwin to refute their theory!

The truth, so far as I can see, is that liberals only love Darwin because they hate those who don't swallow him whole. It makes them feel smart, as if they were somehow scientists themselves, logical and intellectually superior, even if they can't tell the difference between a Bunsen burner and a tiki torch.

So while the snobs of the Left lump all conservatives in with those they regard as ignorant, simple-minded, anonymous oafs, conservatives aim their barbs at the leaders of the opposition — Ivy League-educated twerps like Kerry and Kennedy, Pelosi and Dean, Reid and Leahy, Clinton and Clinton, Boxer and Feinstein, Biden and Byrd. The truth — would you follow any of those dirty dozen into war? Me, I wouldn't even follow them to the buffet table.

• 79 •

I've Got No Big Secrets!

Sometimes I get the idea that I'm the only person in America with nothing to conceal. Especially since 9/11 and the creation of Homeland Security, all of my liberal friends are up in arms over what they see as their loss of privacy. So, while I had never been all that interested in their private lives before, suddenly I'm wondering what it is they're hiding!

Frankly, I just don't get it. Part of the problem, I admit, is that my own life is an open book. I'm not claiming sainthood, understand, it's just that I don't do much. For one thing, I rarely leave the house if I can help it. You can ask my wife. On top of that, I don't use drugs, take part in orgies, or get drunk. Besides, at my age, if I had any secrets, I'd probably forget what they were.

So, my question to all you hand-wringers is, what are you so afraid we're going to find out? I have even heard people voice fear that the government is going to discover what books they're taking out of the library. Well, inasmuch as the city government, which runs the library, already has that information stored in its computer, unless you've been swiping your reading material all along, what exactly is the big deal? Afraid Uncle Sam is going to uncover the fact that you've been reading Danielle Steel and not Aristotle? If it's any consolation, we've suspected it all along.

One can only surmise that such people were caught once as teenagers with a copy of *Playboy* or an illustrated *Moll Flanders* under the mattress and never got over the trauma.

If you really want to send a liberal up the wall, try suggesting that national I.D. numbers are long overdue. Argue that they would provide a way to track down potential terrorists, fugitive criminals, and deadbeat dads, and watch them froth at the mouth.

The point that they ignore — these pompous members of the ACLU who are forever whining, "I'm an individual, not a number" — is that they are actually an endless series of numbers. Just some of which are connected to phones, computers, home and office addresses, Social Security, mortgages, credit cards, insurance policies, and birth certificates. The only things unique about these clowns are their fingerprints.

Yet, somehow they manage to survive in spite of having to cart around all those numbers. What, then, is it about a national I.D. that sets them to quivering like little bowls of Jell-O?

"Big Brother," they'll whisper, their eyes darting around, scanning the horizon for men wearing sunglasses and brown shoes, and whispering into their wristwatches.

These poor souls are obviously textbook cases of paranoia. But what their fears tell us, aside from the fact that they're all as dizzy as poodles, is that they have humongous egos. In fact, if their egos were as heavy as they are large, these people would have to shlep them around in wheelbarrows. I mean, they actually believe that government agencies are tracking them. Right, like the FBI really cares what my cousin, the dentist, thinks about Bush's foreign policy! But the thing that makes me crazy is that these are the very same people who want more money and more power in the hands of the federal government. Liberals, after all, are always opposed to tax cuts because, one assumes, they actually believe the pork barrel crowd in Washington is better equipped to fritter away our money than we are.

So, what it comes down to is that although liberals are only too happy to trust the wise and benevolent politicians to spend trillions of dollars, enact laws, and declare war, they don't trust them not to peek at what library books we're checking out!

• 80 •

Why Dogs, Not Liberals, Are Man's Best Friend

Some people are convinced that a compassionate conservative is an oxymoron. But I know better. I'm not suggesting I am one, but I do know a few. They're the people who occasionally take me to task for being too critical of liberals.

They'll insist that some of their best friends are liberals. Liberals, they'll inform me, make fine neighbors and positively first-rate relatives. I patiently explain that they're preaching to the choir. I know first-hand that liberals can be all of those things, and more.

My only problem with liberals is that they're hypocrites, and they can't help lying.

Perhaps, like my friends, you now think I'm too harsh in my judgment. On the contrary, I think I tend to give liberals the benefit of the doubt. I happen to believe they are so besotted by their emotions that they can't help painting themselves into indefensible corners. To blame a liberal for lying and blatant hypocrisy would be as heartless as blaming an alcoholic for drinking. In fact, I suspect that, like alcoholics, liberals suffer from a chemical imbalance. Otherwise, how would you explain the enormous gulf between what they say and what they do?

For instance, how often have we read newspaper editorials arguing for affirmative action in schools and in the workplace? In most cases, those pieces are not being written or edited by members of a

racial minority group. So, if they were sincere, shouldn't these journalists clear out their desks and surrender their jobs to somewhat
less qualified, but far more deserving, blacks and Hispanics?

Or consider, if you will, how consistently liberals object to tax
cuts. They prattle on incessantly about how much the wealthy benefit, ignoring the logic that if there's a 10% reduction across the
board, it figures that the person who pays more will get more. But,
when liberals blather about the inequities of tax cuts, you realize
they actually believe that if a millionaire saves fifty thousand on his
tax bill, the guy who only earns, say, thirty grand a year should get
the same return!

Liberals, for reasons that some of us will never comprehend, are
convinced that the federal government can be trusted to spend
money more wisely than the people who actually earn it. When Bill
Clinton was in the White House, he said as much.

They're entitled to their beliefs, you say. Where does the inconsistency come in, you ask? It's simply this — liberals spend just as
much money as conservatives on shrewd attorneys and clever
C.P.A.s, attempting to lower their own tax liability. There is nothing
in the tax laws, after all, that prohibits an American citizen from
paying Uncle Sam more than he owes. But, I have yet to hear of a
liberal, even one as rich as George Soros, who claimed that, even
though he belonged in the 35% bracket, he so admired the way in
which Congress spent his money, he was going to pay the I.R.S. 50
or maybe even 60 percent.

Finally, I have never heard a liberal speak out in favor of school
vouchers. Instead, they wave the flag for public schools, even
though everybody in his right mind knows that, in spite of the No
Child Left Behind program, a majority of public schools in America
are a disgrace. The system has routinely passed along youngsters
who wound up graduating from high school lacking self-discipline

and even rudimentary math and reading skills. Yet, every liberal in Congress can be counted on to pay lip service to public education, although not one of them has a child enrolled in the Washington, D.C., school system!

So, while I acknowledge that liberals can be as loyal and steadfast as cocker spaniels, I have found it is nearly impossible to paper-train them.

• 81 •
Liberals and Other Phonies

Some people contend that I always pick on left wingers. That's not true. It is true that I take greater pleasure in attacking Democrats more than I do Republicans, but that's because they are not only wrong on virtually every major issue, but they're hypocrites, to boot. This is especially true of those we know best — the Hollywood variety, the sort of screwballs who lionize the likes of Michael Moore.

What, you have to wonder, is with these people? Are they even aware of the gulf between what they profess and what they do? For example, they are opposed to law-abiding citizens owning guns. But these grossly overpaid high school dropouts have, along with their agents, managers, flacks, and stooges, gun-toting bodyguards on their payroll. In their minds, apparently, guns are only bad when you and I have them.

Hollywood liberals will bore you to death proclaiming their devotion to the environment. But all of them, with the much-publicized exception of Ed Begley, Jr., drive around in gas-guzzling limos, SUVs, and Porsches, and fly in private fuel-guzzling jets. To top things off, they live in mansions so enormous they could provide housing for half the illegal aliens in Los Angeles.

The biggest reason these creeps oppose school vouchers is because they fear that, given the option, many parents would elect to send their children to parochial schools. The only thing these people hate nearly as much as having one of their movies flop at the box office is the whole idea of mainstream religion. From the way they and their favorite organization, the ACLU, feel about

Christianity, you would think that if somebody even pointed a cross in their direction, they'd snarl and back off the way Bela Lugosi did in those old Count Dracula movies.

The mere sight of a Jewish menorah or a Christmas tree in a public park drives them into an absolute frenzy. The one religion these self-deluded loonies will never condemn is Islam. Let some nutty woman in Florida insist it's her religious right as a Muslim to wear a veil in her driver's license photo and they'll plead her case until the cows come home.

There is one subject about which Republicans, at least Republican politicians, are every bit as hypocritical as their Democratic brethren. Namely, public schools. Even though the very rich and very influential teachers union funnels nearly all of its largesse to those on the left, most members of the GOP are too scared to open their yaps. Partly that's because public school education is a sacred topic. A politician might as well attack Santa Claus or motherhood. But there's more to it than that. Hypocrisy, as is so often the case where politicians are concerned, is the single biggest reason that Washingtonians, no matter which party they belong to, maintain their Mafia-like code of silence. And why would that be? The dirty little secret they don't want to have bandied about is that they're elitists, and that not one of their own kids is enrolled in the Washington, D.C., public school system!

Oh, sure, every four years, presidential hopefuls will drop by for photo ops and have their pictures taken with cute little black school children, but that's the extent of it. Don't expect to see them showing up for PTA meetings or bake sales. And, yes, it's true that the families of some representatives don't even reside in the nation's capital, but live back home in the congressional district. But that still doesn't mean their sprouts attend the local junior high. Public schools are the backbone of this nation, the pols will solemnly insist in their pompous speeches, but you can wager dollars to donuts that their sons and daughters are enrolled in pricey prep schools.

I have always found it peculiar that politicians like to refer to themselves as public servants. However, in old English movies, which is the only place that most of us came across maids and butlers, it was always said of even the best of them that they knew their place. Isn't it odd that our own servants always assume their place is at the head of the line?

• 82 •

The Most Obnoxious Group in America

I am not a religious man. I'm neither proud of that nor ashamed. I merely state that fact to establish where I'm coming from. I have friends who are believers and friends who are not. Where religion is concerned, I believe in live and let live. I only wish that the ACLU shared that attitude. I don't like to describe myself as an agnostic or an atheist because I don't care to align myself with the people whose own religion consists of a profound antipathy to everybody else's.

I decided a long time ago that religion would play no part in my life, but I felt no compulsion to convert others. Oddly enough, I never resented the folks who would ring my doorbell and try to proselytize me. Although I don't like dealing with uninvited guests, I always thought it was nice of them to be that concerned about the eternal soul of a perfect stranger.

Having said all that, I wish to announce that I despise the ACLU for its relentless attacks on Christianity and Judaism. It's bad enough that they will wage battle on behalf of any busybody looking to banish Christmas and Hanukah symbols from public places, including one's own front yard. However, these very same lawyers will eagerly go to the mat to safeguard a Muslim's right to wear a disguise on her driver's license, a Navajo's right to smoke peyote, and a cultist's right to ritualistically slaughter small animals.

The ACLU proclaims that they're merely abiding by the Constitution's insistence on the separation of church and state. The only problem with that position is that the Constitution says no such thing. Although the secular Left has glommed on to that catch phrase like a pitbull gnawing on a shinbone, the First Amendment simply states: "Congress shall make no law respecting establishment of religion, or prohibiting the free exercise thereof."

That is a far cry from forcing apartment dwellers to remove holiday wreaths from their door or insisting that communities remove Nativity scenes from parks or compelling small towns to change "Christmas Holiday" in their high school calendars to "Winter Break."

The problem with the ACLU is that it is composed in equal measure of self-righteous fools and fascistic bullies. Because so many of their members are rich and privileged, they will, on the one hand, blather on about their love of democracy, while, at the same time, assume they alone know what's best for everyone else.

Because they are so out of step with the majority, they can rarely have their way via a democratic ballot. There are, in fact, only two means by which they ever have their way. The first is by getting liberal judges to set aside election results, as they have done over such issues as capital punishment, illegal immigration, and affirmative action. The second way is by intimidating those — be they individuals, cities or organizations — that lack the backbone or the financial wherewithal to defend themselves against the ACLU's mob of shysters.

If the authors of the Constitution had ever, in their worst nightmares, envisioned a group as vile as the ACLU, I feel certain that they would have rephrased the First Amendment to read: "Congress shall make no law respecting establishment of religion, or prohibiting the free exercise thereof. Period! And we're not kidding, so help us God!"

• 83 •

Psychoanalyzing the Loony Left

Sigmund Freud was the fellow who had the copyright on the ego, the id, and the superego. He was also the guy who managed to turn the couch, formerly just another piece of overstuffed Viennese furniture, into a legitimate business expense. But even he acknowledged that he was unable to decipher what it was that women wanted.

Strangely enough, that happens to be one question to which I actually know the answer. Women want men to be manly chaps, strong and virile, while at the same time they want us to be completely open and in touch with our emotions. Furthermore, they want us to be more interested in what they think, say, and feel than we are in cars, sports, and beer. In short, they want the impossible. The more reasonable among them will settle for our picking up after ourselves.

The thing that has me stumped is trying to figure out what leftists want. For example, when left-wing judges take it upon themselves to legislate from the bench, liberals are quick to say that the Constitution is a living document and that it has to evolve to accommodate a changing world. However, whenever a conservative suggests that the Fourteenth Amendment, which grants automatic citizenship on any person born in America, ought to be changed in order to deny that gift to those born to illegal aliens, those same people carry on as if the Constitution, like the Ten Commandments, was carved in stone.

But, really, we have no reason to believe that the Founding Fathers, who fought a war in order to gain sovereignty for this nation, wouldn't have entertained second thoughts if they'd ever envisioned a foreign invasion numbering in the millions. I mean, it's a basic tenet of the law that nobody is entitled to profit from a crime. To suggest that the child, the beneficiary of his parents' illegal act, doesn't profit is patently absurd. To argue that he shouldn't be deprived of the advantage because he didn't break the law is ridiculous. You might as well suggest that if a bank robber gives his ill-gotten gains to his wife and kids, the family should get to keep the loot because, after all, they weren't the ones who drove the getaway car.

Another thing about liberals I can't begin to figure out is their abiding devotion to failed economic theories. The fact that communism hasn't worked anywhere in the world doesn't cool their ardor in the slightest. The fact that Marx's brainstorm invariably metasta-sizes into a despotic tyranny — be it in the Soviet Union, China, Cuba, Cambodia, or Venezuela — doesn't make the slightest impres-sion on them. Neither does the fact that socialism has brought much of Europe to the brink of moral and financial bankruptcy faze them in the least.

In our own country, the most obvious failure of socialism is Social Security, the single largest pyramid scheme ever conceived by the mind of man. When Ponzi did it, he went to jail for fraud; when Roosevelt pulled it off, he was hailed as a savior. As someone or other once observed, if you're going to steal, steal big.

So why is it that leftists continue to promote these half-cocked alternatives to capitalism, the only economic program that's ever motivated people to aspire, to compete, to achieve, and to innovate?

Well, I hate to be impolite, but when people keep doing the same thing in spite of getting the same rotten results, we have been told by experts in the field that it's a pretty sure sign of insanity.

And just in case any doubt remains, you merely have to look to those who speak on their behalf. Assuming you're not a cuckoo yourself, can you possibly imagine rallying around the unappetizing likes of Gore and Kerry, Schumer and Durbin, Kennedy and Rangel, Leahy and Biden, Byrd and Boxer, Sharpton and Jackson, McKinney and Waters, Al Franken and Michael Moore, George Soros and Norman Lear, Hillary and Bill, and Jimmy Carter?

Or merely consider the man the liberals selected to be their party's leader, the man they chose to carry their banner into battle. While most people will always associate Howard Dean with his primary election meltdown, I chose to give him the benefit of the doubt. After all, in the heat of a presidential campaign — especially a campaign in which he had somehow managed to snatch defeat from the very jaws of victory — people are given to saying, or, in Dean's case, shrieking some very odd things.

Instead, my clearest, most lasting memory of the party boss will forever be his calm and collected response to someone's asking what the Democratic candidates should be saying in the upcoming elections. Replied Mr. Dean: "My three-word message is, we can do better."

Chapter Fourteen

STILL MORE JETSAM

• 84 •
Pooh-Bahs and Moolah

When a politician speaks, there are two things he will invariably lie about. The first is that he wants to get money out of the election process. What he really wants is to get money out of his opponent's election process.

Politicians claim it's demeaning to ask people for campaign funds. Well, not entirely. For one thing, fundraising events allow politicians to hog the spotlight and to hobnob with show business celebrities. For another, in what other endeavor do people — often perfect strangers — contribute their hard-earned money to keep another person gainfully employed? That's pretty heady stuff. Imagine having a $500-a-plate dinner held in your honor and having movie stars show up for bad chicken, stale rolls, and a fruit cup, just to hear you talk about yourself. Believe me, you don't get your ego massaged that way if you sell insurance or work at the widget factory. Only pols expect their fellow Americans to volunteer time and money to help them get or keep a job. What a deal! And what a job! When you're at work, you spend most of your time deciding how to spend other people's money. And when you're not working, you're flying around the world on junkets passed off as fact-finding missions. And instead of being treated like the spongers they are, they get standing ovations from adoring throngs and get to see their faces plastered on the cover of *Time*. The other big lie you hear from these shmoes is that they favor smaller government and less bureaucracy. Take it from me, no politician wants less power. They may disagree among themselves as to how to spend your tax dollars, but every last one of them thinks he would spend your money far more wisely than you would. As for their desire to eliminate bureaucrats, you might as well believe that the Pentagon wants a smaller Army. Politicians measure their own power and prestige by the number of bureaucrats they oversee. It's called patronage. In Washington, it passes for mother's milk. And although I am a conservative, I regret to say that Republicans are no different from Democrats when it comes to such basic matters as money, ego, and influence. They are just as likely to ignore U.S. sovereignty by granting amnesty to illegals as they go trolling for Hispanic votes, and argue for affirmative action as they go whoring for black votes. When you get right down to it, there's one sure way to tell when a politician is lying. Just check to see if his mouth is moving.

• 85 •
China: Least-Favored Nation

I don't, as a rule, spend a lot of time feeling sorry for China. But that was before I read about the problems that nation is already having as Beijing gears up to host the 2008 Olympics. I'm not referring to the usual headaches suffered by host cities, such as building all those pricey sports venues that will never be used again, getting the bums out of sight, and schooling their cab drivers in the best way to turn a tourist's two-mile taxi ride into a cross-country excursion.

No, China's problem has the charm of at least being unique. It appears that the one thing that most of her 1.2 billion citizens have in common is that they're rude, crude, and darn proud of it.

Stalin's Soviet Union was always announcing ambitious five-year plans for industry and agriculture, invariably failing to realize any of them except in their dreams and their propaganda. Based on what I've been reading about Chinese behavior, their three-year plan is likewise doomed to failure.

It seems that the Chinese who, in the past, were famous for their dignified ways, have turned into a nation of boors. Not too surprisingly, they have super role model Mao Tse-tung to blame for it.

According to Edgar Snow, author of *Red Star Over China,* Mao was known to scratch himself wherever and whenever he felt like it, to remove his clothes and conduct meetings naked when the temperature rose, and to "absent-mindedly" open his fly, searching for lice and fleas. Frankly, if the man was known to attend meetings in his birthday suit, I don't know why Mr. Snow would assume that

Mao was being absent-minded when he went hunting for those pesky mites.

In 1954, we're told, Mao met former British Prime Minister Clement Attlee while wearing pants that were patched on the butt. When one of his aides had suggested that he might wish to wear a new pair of trousers for the occasion, Mao replied, "Who will look at my behind?" Admittedly, it's the sort of thing I say to my wife whenever she suggests I change my pants, shirt, shoes, or jacket before we go out, but Mao, being Mao, got away with it. It's good to be dictator.

Flush with the success of that earlier fashion statement, in 1972, Mao attended the funeral of Marshall Chen Yi in his pajamas. I must confess that while Mao was alive, I always assumed he was an old sober sides, never even suspecting that inside that fat man a skinny man named Groucho Marx was screaming to get out.

Is it any wonder that with Mao setting the standards, today China is full of people who not only spit, but regularly urinate on the sidewalk. Butting in line is also commonplace, as is cooking on the street, which is also the favorite venue for fistfights.

In 1949, when the Communists took power, etiquette wasn't merely sloughed aside, it was rooted out and sent packing. Refinement was seen as a plot by the former ruling class to keep the lower class in its place.

However, when during a basketball game last July a Chinese player was fouled by a member of the Puerto Rican team, a small riot ensued, the crowd behaving in a way we have come to associate with English soccer hooligans and Oakland Raider football fans.

That served as a wake-up call for the government, suddenly envisioning more of the same or worse three short years down the road, when all the world's eyes would be on Beijing.

Of course, it's not just the Olympics that is motivating China to clean up its image. It's also a matter of good business. It appears that, in spite of turning out all those cheap goods, Chinese business-men and their employees are so rude, undependable, and unethical, many American and European companies are loath to do business with them.

As a result, China is fostering a nationwide improvement pro-gram that includes TV shows, slogans, university courses, and even competitions between cities, all intended to replace Mao with Miss Manners.

In Beijing alone, 100,000 municipal workers are being trained to smile, bathe, and to wear socks to work. I'm guessing that one of the more popular slogans reminds one and all that Rome wasn't built in a day.

In addition, June Yamada, author of an etiquette bestseller called *Tell It Like It Is, June,* has opened an academy devoted to improving social conduct. Because she also works outside her academy, on a recent weekend, she was training the sales staff at a high-end jewelry store. During several hours of role-playing, she instructed them to be warm and polite and to stop doggedly following customers around the store as if they were all well-known jewel thieves.

Well, I, for one, wish China well. Even if they are a bunch of rot-ten Commies, it can't hurt to have them at least become polite rotten Commies.

Plus, I was thinking, when her gig over there is finished, maybe we can persuade Ms. Yamada to come here and whip our salespeo-ple into shape.

• 86 •

Happy Cesar Chavez Day

From everything I've heard and read, Cesar Chavez was a wonderful man. I'm not just saying that, either. I just want to make it clear that I have nothing against him, personally. But another state holiday, for crying out loud! I don't even want to get into the cost in tax dollars for these paid vacations. But surely enough is enough, already.

We are told that Senor Chavez is the first Latino so honored here in California. He may be the first, but I can assure you, with the fast-growing number of Hispanics in the state, he won't be the last. After all, it doesn't cost the legislators anything to cast these gutless votes, and if it makes a large bloc of the electorate happy, they can but hope that the gratitude carries over to the next election. Today, Cesar Chavez; tomorrow, Ricardo Montalban.

It doesn't even make sense that the occasion of Cesar Chavez's birthday be the reason a multitude of state employees get the day off. Possibly I could see where an argument could be made for the farm workers to throw a party, but the clerks at the DMV?!

Besides, the whole point behind Chavez's crusade was that honest work should be rewarded with decent wages. So, in honor of the work ethic, everybody gets to knock off and go to the beach?

But then I always thought it odd that the greatest honor that could be bestowed on the American labor movement was that for an entire day, nobody in the country would perform any labor, except maybe barbecue a few burgers.

Knowing people as I do, I am willing to bet that some of you are dismissing my remarks as those of a curmudgeon and a crank. Some of you, I'd wager, are writing off my argument as a case of, pardon the expression, sour grapes. You're positive I'd be whistling a whole different tune if the California State Legislature had voted to make January 5th Burt Prelutsky Day. Okay, I won't deny it. But it's certainly not for the petty reasons you assume. It just seems logical that if several hundred thousand people are going to get the day off, it shouldn't be in honor of hard work, but in tribute to sloth.

• 87 •
The Usual Suspects

Like most people, I had long wondered about the identity of Deep Throat. Now that W. Mark Felt has stepped forward confessing to having been Mr. Throat, I can scratch the two likeliest suspects from my short list. That would be Richard Nixon and me. I suppose some explanation is required.

For openers, I never for a moment suspected Alexander Haig. He always loved the spotlight far too much to hide in the shadows, lurking in parking structures, whispering secrets to Robert Woodward and Carl Bernstein.

I had a couple of reasons for thinking that President Nixon had orchestrated his own downfall. The reasons, in no particular order, were financial and psychological. At some point, following his eight years as vice president, he took a half million dollar deduction on his income taxes after donating his papers to some institution or other. The IRS demurred as only they can. I think they valued the vice presidential papers at about $1.49, and then insisted that Mr. Nixon cough up the difference.

The way I saw it — this being long before the time when people like the Clintons could expect multimillion-dollar book deals once they vacated the White House — Nixon decided he'd play it cagier the second time around. How better to make certain that his presidential papers would have an inflated value than by making certain he wasn't just another run-of-the-mill ex-president, but the very first one to be ridden out of office on a rail?!

My other theory had to do with the nature of the man. Unlike most successful politicians who use the public the way the rest of us use a roaring fire — to warm ourselves — Nixon always seemed estranged from people. Where other politicians try to generate heat, he generated cold. He never seemed at ease in public. Even in that famous photo of Nixon strolling on the beach at San Clemente, the man wore a suit and tie. He was the absolute antithesis of President Kennedy. Kennedy was Jack to millions; Nixon was always Richard, never Dick, except when people needed a rhyme for tricky.

Nixon was the man who after losing the 1962 California gubernatorial race to Pat Brown announced that he was bowing out of public life and chided the members of the media, telling them that they'd no longer have Nixon to kick around anymore. Six years later, he was president of the United States, making himself out to be not only a liar, but a false prophet.

Now if you are even the slightest bit paranoid, as Nixon often appeared to be, imagine the internal conflict that must have taken place every morning when he woke up in the White House and discovered that it wasn't all a dream. How could he reconcile his belief that everyone was out to get him with the fact that he had twice been elected leader of the most powerful nation on earth? The strain had to have been unbearable. He must constantly have been wondering when the other shoe was going to drop and his enemies would leap out of the closet like bogeymen and hound him out of the Oval Office.

So, to me, it made sense if he finally decided to take matters into his own hands and end his torment. The bonus would have been that when the movie came out, he'd get to see tall, good-looking Hal Holbrook playing him in *All the President's Men.*

Now you're probably wondering how my other suspect could possibly be yours truly. Well, for openers, just about everyone in America at the time was being suspected, except me. Needless to say, if you read any mysteries at all, that's a big red flag. The guilty party is always the last person you'd guess. The other thing is, back in the early '70s, I used to drink a lot. Some mornings I'd wake up and barely remember anything at all. So, how could I be sure I wasn't spending some of those evenings telling secrets to Woodward and Bernstein?

• 88 •
Moms Make Lousy Dads

One of the more fatuous beliefs that has been foisted off by self-proclaimed feminists and other politically correct lamebrains is that children don't really need fathers. I used to say that American women, thanks to increased salaries and well-stocked sperm banks, had reached a point where they only needed men to open ketchup bottles and get stuff down from high shelves. Ladies, I was joking!

I had no idea that so many women took the line to heart. Thanks to my good joke and Gloria Steinem's bad one — that crack about fish needing bicycles — women have become increasingly wacky. What is really surprising, considering that thirty years of feminist propaganda has promoted the natural superiority of females, is how masculine, in the worst sense of the word, so many women have become.

Surely I am not the only person who has noticed that these days young women are just as likely as men to smoke, to get bombed on booze and cuss in public, and perhaps even likelier to drive like maniacs and to flip you off for daring to share the road with them.

In the business world, far too many women salivate at the thought of being regarded as cold and ruthless. They are every bit as likely to torment and humiliate their employees and to promote an atmosphere of fear and anger, especially among their female underlings. Call these women cut-throat and they think you're trying to sweet talk them.

Perhaps it's simply a case of Stockholm syndrome gone amok. As you probably know, that's a situation in which hostages come to identify not with their rescuers, but with their captors. Women, in their own defense, might possibly claim that they'd been powerless for so long that it was inevitable that they'd take on the very characteristics they've despised. But that's a load of hooey. I say if you're going to behave like an idiot and a bully, don't make excuses for your boorishness. God knows men don't!

Inasmuch as more and more women are eager to hand off their offspring to a nanny, a granny or a nursery school, you have to wonder why most of them even bother giving birth. All they seem to have to show for the experience are stretch marks.

In a society that is determined to accept the nutty notion that two gay men or a pair of lesbians are just as likely — they really mean likelier— to raise a normal, healthy child as a married man and woman, how could anybody dare suggest that a single woman isn't equally capable? Well, she isn't. This is especially true when the child is a boy. No matter how hard she tries, no matter how much she cares, no matter how many broken nails she's willing to sacrifice in order to play catch with the kid, the bottom line is she's a woman. And just because so many of the morons in Hollywood have turned single motherhood into another fad, sort of like collagen lips and plastic bosoms, doesn't make it a good idea.

It simply makes sense that a boy needs a man in his life to act as a role model, to show him not only how to curb his temper and to temper his testosterone, but also how to avoid being feminized into something resembling a well-dressed eunuch.

The point I am looking to make I saw made perfectly in a segment of a TV magazine show some years ago. It seems that in Africa, on a game preserve, the rangers were discovering the mutilated carcasses of several rhinos. They couldn't determine who was responsible for the carnage, and they couldn't imagine a motive.

After conducting an investigation, they found to their amazement that a band of teenage elephants was killing the rhinos for no other reason than that they felt like it. It was their version of drive-by shootings. Like our own urban gangs, the young rogues even had a leader.

The rangers thought long and hard about the problem. The first thing they realized was that the teenagers were free to make up their own evil rules of behavior because, like the bloodthirsty kids in *Lord of the Flies,* there were no adults in their world. All the bull elephants had been slaughtered by poachers for their ivory.

Then, because they didn't have to answer to politicians or social workers, the rangers did two essential things. First, having determined he was incorrigible, they killed the leader of the pack. Next, they flew in several bull elephants. In no time at all, order was restored. The big guys let it be known that if there was any more rhino-stomping, there would be hell to pay. Their message was short and sweet; namely that elephants don't behave that way.

So, for all their professional advances, there are still a few things that women simply can't do as well as men. Some of those things, such as throwing a football forty yards in a perfect spiral or crushing a beer can on their forehead, aren't all that essential. Important, I'll grant you, but not absolutely essential to society at large. However, when it comes to rearing male children, we'd all probably be better off if the ladies simply dropped the kids off in the woods for wolves to raise.

• 89 •
A Few Immodest Proposals

Because the entire process of appointing Supreme Court justices has become so politicized, many people would like to see the job description changed to include term limits. They seem to think that things would get better if, instead of lifetime sinecures, the justices would be limited to, say, ten or twelve-year appointments. Frankly, I'm of two minds on the subject. It all depends on whom we're talking about. I'm certainly in no hurry to give Scalia and Thomas the boot, whereas in the case of Souter and Ginsburg, I'd gladly help them pack and drive them to the airport.

There's another radical notion floating around these days. It seems the Democrats think it would be a swell idea to impeach President Bush. They seem to think he's been overzealous in waging the war on terrorism. I disagree with them. As I see it, if they're wrong, we could all be killed by Islamic fanatics; if Bush is wrong, somebody in the FBI might discover I just checked Somerset Maugham's *Theatre* out of the public library.

I don't happen to believe the president has broken any laws. It's also my belief that his enemies would be just as willing to impeach him for jaywalking or splitting an infinitive if they could pull it off. I understand. That's politics. The thing I can't figure out about this plan of theirs is whether they are totally unaware of the rules of succession as spelled out in Article 2 of the Constitution, or if they really like Dick Cheney as much as I do.

Although I am undecided about term limits when it comes to federal judges, it's a whole other matter when it comes to senators.

And forget term limits, I'd do away with them entirely. What purpose do they serve? What do those hundred buffoons do that couldn't be handled just as ineptly by that crowd of stiffs in the House?

When our forefathers were setting things up, they sought a way to balance things out so that the smaller states wouldn't be totally overwhelmed by those states with much greater populations. But let's face it, it's a notion whose time has come and gone. Among them, Alaska, Delaware, North Dakota, South Dakota, Vermont and Wyoming have about as many people as Kentucky, but they have 12 senators, while Kentucky only has two. And Kentucky has only about a tenth the population of California. Does that seem fair? It sounds downright un-American to me.

Besides, if we got rid of all that senatorial deadwood, we'd save a bloody fortune. I'm not just talking about their salaries and pensions, either. Every single one of them, even those who complain the most about the pork in the federal budget, controls a virtual fiefdom that would have made an old French nobleman drool with envy. Ted Kennedy, alone, has more courtiers and assorted flunkies waiting on him than Louis XVI ever dreamed of; and as with Louis, it's the poor taxpayers who are footing the bill.

Before dismissing my idea out of hand, pause just a moment and picture life without Charles Schumer, Robert Byrd, Richard Durbin, Harry Reid, Patrick Leahy, Barbara Boxer, Dianne Feinstein, Joe Biden, and Hillary Clinton.

I don't know about the rest of you, but the mere thought of a world in which John Kerry would be just another aging gigolo is enough to make me swoon.

I realize that along with the absolute dregs of humanity I just listed, I'd be eliminating employment for a handful of decent conservatives. But that's okay. I can live with it. I say the fewer politicians of any political stripe, the better.

A bright fellow named Paul Rinderle wrote to me recently, suggesting that the moral arc of a Washington career could be divided into four parts: idealism, pragmatism, ambition, and, ultimately, corruption.

I wrote back to say that, by and large, I agreed with his analysis. I just felt it was a shame that the typical politician went through all four stages in a single afternoon.

• 90 •
Generation Gaps

Recently, I heard some author being interviewed on the radio. It was his contention that the generation of baby boomers was greater than the earlier one that had had to contend with the Great Depression and World War II. He based his belief on the fact that it was the boomers who had brought about civil rights for blacks and equal rights for women.

I, myself, find it difficult to compare the accomplishments and sacrifices of one group of Americans against another. But I suppose if you double-dared me to label any generation as the greatest, I would cast my vote for the one that not only waged war against the world's greatest superpower, but also found the time and inspiration to forge a new nation based on the Declaration of Independence and the U.S. Constitution.

My major problem with the boomers is that they were the most arrogant, self-congratulatory group in American history. And what's more, they bred such selfish, self-centered offspring, you'd think they were all members of the English royal family.

Even though the nation had been around for 200 years, it took all that time before large numbers of American youngsters came to believe they were exceptional and deserved unbridled admiration for no other reason than that they existed.

It was only natural that coupled with that feeling of personal entitlement would be the belief that a level playing field was supposed to ensure equal results. The idea that some people are simply smarter, more disciplined, and motivated was dismissed as elitist thinking. If Bobby got better grades, then went to a better college, got a superior education, and therefore wound up with a better job than Billy, it wasn't because Bobby had studied harder and goofed off less, it could only be explained on the basis of racism.

In much the same way, the part of the Declaration of Independence that mentioned the pursuit of happiness was re-interpreted to mean that happiness was guaranteed to one and all, and that its pursuit was a catch-all that could be used to justify abortions on demand, gay marriages, and even, according to NAMBLA, pedophilia.

We are also so spoiled that we believe we are entitled to pay half as much for gas as they pay in parts of Europe. Still, many of those complaining the loudest when the price goes up a dime a gallon are those who refuse to even consider drilling in Alaska. The way these yahoos carry on about destroying the Godforsaken environment in the frozen tundra, you'd think we were talking about erecting oil derricks on Park, Michigan, or Pennsylvania avenues.

It so happens, however, that I have two nifty plans for lowering the price of gas. My first notion is to invade Saudi Arabia and confiscate its oil fields. Then all those pinheads who said that Bush shouldn't attack Iraq because, whereas Hussein had no connection to 9/11, most of the terrorists hailed from Saudi Arabia, would have to shut up.

Plan B is that we stop buying oil from other countries and start using our gigantic reserves. The rest of the world is always complaining that America uses too much petroleum. Fine. So let Russia, Mexico, Venezuela, and the Arab countries see how they like it when we actually stop buying just about the only thing they have to sell. It seems to me that the tail's been wagging the dog for far too long. If the U.S. said that $30-a-barrel was as much as we were willing to pay, I suspect the oil producers would cut each other's throat to meet our price and become our major supplier.

It figures that if you're Wal-Mart, you get a better price and faster delivery from the factories than if you're Charley's Five-and Dime in Duluth. So why shouldn't America decide what we're willing to pay instead of leaving it up to a bunch of shmoes we wouldn't even want to have lunch with?

The really nice thing about Plan B is that it doesn't preclude our also going with Plan A.

· 91 ·

Sex in America

Back when Bill Clinton was leaving his mark on history by leaving his mark on Monica Lewinsky's dress, one of the most aggravating aspects of the entire shabby episode was having our nation being patronized by the European media. As usual, the snidest commentary came to us courtesy of the French.

They were like 80 million cats lapping up cream. Our alleged lack of sophistication is like food and drink to them. They couldn't stop snickering over our bourgeois value system. After all, their premier had a mistress. What real man didn't? It's to be expected. Only people as backward as Americans would make a fuss over something so natural. All the while, the French ignored the fact that Clinton had committed perjury, which many of us took far more seriously than whether he had cheated on Hillary. Feeling as we did about his wife, that struck many of us as perfectly reasonable.

But, much as I hate doing it, I'm afraid I have to admit that, for once, the French aren't entirely off base. While I regard Clinton as a national albatross for a variety of reasons quite aside from his having sex with a young intern, I happen to think that where sex is concerned, Americans are, by and large, childish and embarrassing.

For instance, consider that for millions of us, the computer age with its magnificent superhighway of information translates into a multi-billion-dollar pornography industry. I mean, let's face facts — when people object so strenuously to the portions of the Patriot Act that permit the feds to eavesdrop on our computers, what do you think it is that makes them so darn nervous? That the world will discover that they've been checking up on the annual rainfall in the Amazon rain forest or finding out Millard Fillmore's middle name?

Sometimes, I swear, people are so daffy when it comes to things even slightly sexual that I almost feel like donning a beret, lighting up a stinky cigarette, and snorting through my nose.

I'll mention just a few things, and you decide whether or not we're a nation of goofballs. First, there's the fact that Paris Hilton, a woman of rather ordinary looks and no discernible talent, became famous simply because a video of her having sex with some guy became public property.

Next, there's the annual swimsuit issue of *Sports Illustrated.* Every week, *SI* is jam-packed with extremely well-written and well-photographed articles dealing with the world of athletics. Then, once a year, they devote a cover and a few pages to photos of pretty girls modeling bikinis, and you get the idea the end of the world is nigh. Now keep in mind that *Playboy* has been displaying even prettier girls in and out of bikinis for about 50 years. Still, every year, as predictably as the swallows returning to Capistrano, you can count on pundits endlessly kicking the topic around in newspapers and on talk shows. What's more, if I could collect twenty-five bucks for every Sunday sermon in which some minister pondered whether this marked the end of western civilization, I could run out and buy a new car.

At least the women in *Sports Illustrated* are gorgeous and voluptuous. They are, after all, hired specifically for their good looks. But a few years ago, we were all witness to something that should have served as a wake-up call. A woman's soccer team had just won a big match. Their star player, Brandi Chastain, celebrated the victory by pulling off her blouse and running around the field. If you recall, she wasn't naked. She was wearing a sports bra, which in the world of lingerie is comparable to your grandmother's bloomers. What's more, Ms. Chastain, a fine soccer player and probably a nice person, is as flat as an ironing board. But the way that America carried on, you'd have thought that the woman had pulled a Lady Godiva and gone riding nude, at high noon, through the center of town.

Why, you ask, is this so important? Because it behooves us all not to supply the French with artillery with which they can mock us. Which, when you get right down to it, is the only sort of artillery the French ever actually use.

• 92 •
Down with the Independent Voter

Mainly because President Bush and his Republican cohorts are so wishy-washy when it comes to the plague of illegal aliens, I am hearing from a lot of disgruntled conservatives who are threatening to vote for Democrats in November.

I suspect that not too many of them will actually carry out their threat to cut off their nose to spite their face. But I do believe that if the Republican congressmen and senators continue to play follow-the-leader with the lemming who presently occupies the White House, come November, conservative voters will stay home in droves.

As foolish and as gutless as I consider the Republicans to be on this hot button issue, I will not throw away my vote by pretending that there isn't a scintilla of difference between the two parties. That is why I have never understood people who proudly announced they were Independents, just as I can't imagine why anyone elects to go through life voting for Libertarians or Green Party candidates. Why not just hang a sign around your neck declaring yourself to be totally inconsequential?

These folks claim they're sending a message, but when, in election after election, your candidates are lucky if they garner one percent of the vote, what message do you imagine you're sending? The one that's coming through is that whereas the symbols of the two major parties are the donkey and the elephant, yours might as well be the flea.

I realize that those who wish to identify with a third party regard themselves as extremely sophisticated, unwilling to align themselves with parties they regard as the political equivalents of Tweedledum and Tweedledee. In my opinion, they're not sophisticated, merely frustrated. They dislike the compromises, the lobbying, and the trade-offs that go with politics in America. While I don't entirely blame them, I do regard them as hopelessly naïve.

The fact of the matter is that although every Republican is not a true blue conservative, and every Democrat isn't a knee-jerk liberal, there remains a world of difference between the two groups.

Republicans believe in lower taxes because they have enough sense to recognize that the economy flourishes and jobs are created when businesses don't see their profits sucked off by the bureaucrats in Washington. Democrats want taxes increased because it's mother's milk to them. By controlling the money supply, they are able to conduct social engineering on a massive scale.

Republicans believe in a strong military, whereas Democrats place their faith in the U.N.

Republicans believe in legal gun ownership, capital punishment, the three-strikes law, mandatory life sentences for child molesters, English as an official language, and a wall between us and Mexico. Democrats believe there's no difference between your owning a gun and a gang member's owning one. They oppose capital punishment, but are in favor of bilingual education, open borders, and ballots printed in a hundred different languages.

Republicans believe in private property, while Democrats believe municipalities have every right to take away your house and business and hand them over to some other guy so long as he promises to increase the tax base by building a mini-mall on the site you once called home.

Republicans believe we are at war with Islamic fascists. Democrats believe there's a lot to be said for the other side.

Republicans think this is the greatest country on the face of the earth. Democrats think that honor belongs to France.

Republicans think Ronald Reagan was a great president. Democrats think Carter and Clinton were. They also have good things to say about Fidel Castro and Hugo Chavez. There just seems to be something about the letter "C" that strikes a chord with them.

Having said all that, I must admit that I dislike Independents more than I do Democrats because at least I know where liberals stand. But when people tell me they don't vote for the party, they vote for the man, I experience the same queasy sensation as when I used to suffer from acid-reflux.

To me, it's the height of arrogance for any of us to claim to know the man or woman based on what we get from TV. If you actually think you know George W. Bush or John McCain or Hillary Clinton, you're fooling yourself. Every high-profile politician has been manufactured and sold through pretty much the same process that Madison Avenue employs to peddle a bar of soap or a bottle of beer.

Back in the days when Hollywood moguls ran the studios, they used to create stars in the same manner. If women looked and sounded a certain way, they would be typecast as wives and mothers, while others would enjoy careers as hookers, molls, and home-wreckers. What they were like in real life never entered into the equation. The same, of course, held true for the male leads. Sissies were often cast as tough guys, while heels were cast as heroes.

I vote the straight Republican ticket, not because I think the GOP is filled with great statesmen, but because, when all is said and done, I never want Democrats in a position to appoint federal judges. That's the legacy that lingers long after the scoundrels have retired or gone on to that big pork barrel in the sky. The way I see it, one Ruth Bader Ginsburg in a lifetime is one too many!

• 93 •
The Two Americas

Some cynics insist that there are no longer standards in our society. I disagree. We have plenty of standards, but they're double standards. For instance, there's one for blacks and one for whites, one for Christians and another for Muslims and atheists, one for conservatives and one for liberals.

For instance, if a white person speaks critically even about black thugs, crack dealers, and unwed teenagers, he's immediately tarred as a racist. Blacks, on the other hand, are not only free to denounce whites, but they're lionized for their efforts. Recently, a black ex-professor, while on a panel at Howard University's law school, claimed that whites had a plan to kill blacks — and the only solution to the problem was for blacks to exterminate the entire white race. C-Span saw fit to broadcast his insane diatribe, sharing his hate speech with its worldwide audience. Can you in your wildest dreams imagine their covering a Klan convention? No, neither can I.

Every black minister can count on being trotted out for photo ops every time a Democrat runs for dog catcher, but let a white parson speak out on an issue, and leftists start running around, screaming about separation of church and state.

If a Christian wears a cross in the workplace, the ACLU will be only too happy to nail his hide to the wall of the nearest courthouse. But let a twenty-year-old Muslim with a Syrian passport be searched at the airport, and the liberals will hold a candlelight vigil in his honor.

Another obvious example of double standards can be seen in the way the major media reacts to misdeeds, depending upon whether they're committed by those on the left or the right. For example, ever since the election of 2000, the media has been all atwitter about Cheney's connection to Halliburton, but the fact that Bill Clinton was on more intimate terms with Communist China than he was with Monica Lewinsky barely caused a ripple of indignation at *The New York Times* or the *Washington Post.*

Besides which, Halliburton, in case you hadn't noticed, was doing better during the 1990s with a Democrat in the White House than it's done with Cheney just a heartbeat away from the presidency.

Or compare the brouhaha over I. Lewis Libby to the reaction to Sandy Berger's destroying those classified documents he swiped from the National Archives. The way the media sharks are circling Mr. Libby, you'd think he'd sold nuclear secrets to North Korea. Mr. Berger, on the other hand, who should be serving a long sentence at Leavenworth, received a slap on the wrist which essentially ensures that for the next three years he better not even think about shoving classified papers down his pants. And nobody in the major media raised a stink about his getting slapped with the equivalent of a parking ticket.

Something else that politicians on the left get away with is the pretense that they're just a bunch of regular guys and gals representing average Americans. Whenever I hear one of these millionaires trying to pass himself off as an average Joe, I'm reminded that some years ago, when sponsors fell under the spell of demographics and decided they wanted to target only a specific segment of the population, the TV networks naturally followed suit. Then, in order to program shows aimed at the young urban audience that Madison Avenue hankered after, the networks all hired young urbanites to fill the executive suites. So, if the Democratic party is truly dedicated to representing the poor and the downtrodden, how is it that their leadership, both inside and outside the Beltway, is composed entirely of fat cats like Kennedy, Boxer, Dean, Feinstein, the Clintons, the Kerrys, George Soros, and Michael Moore? And why doesn't Senator Schumer, otherwise known as the mouth without a brain attached, start the ball rolling by resigning and handing his job over to a nice homeless person?

But, then, you've probably noticed that when the liberals in politics, the media, and academe promote affirmative action programs based on race and pigmentation, it's never their own jobs they're anxious to hand over to blacks and Hispanics.

As you see, we have plenty of standards. It's honesty and integrity that are, as usual, in pathetically short supply.

Chapter Fifteen

MY LIFE, AND WELCOME TO IT

• 94 •

Proud to Be a Conservative

The other day I was listening to a talk radio show, and heard a caller announce that there's no freedom of speech in this country, that, because of the fascistic administration in Washington, people are afraid to criticize the government. His proof was that Cindy Sheehan had been rebuked for merely exercising her constitutional right to mouth off against authority figures. The show's host correctly pointed out that the First Amendment guarantees her freedom to speak her mind, such as it is, but that doesn't in any way curtail the right of other Americans to call her an idiot.

What the host didn't point out was that even as the caller spoke, he was contradicting his own statement. He was freely sharing his own foolish thoughts with millions of listeners.

Liberals have become so accustomed to having only their own points of view disseminated by the mass media that they now believe that any opinion in conflict with their own is an infringement on their right to free speech. So not only do they feel entitled to spout off ad nauseum, but honest disagreement is regarded as censorship!

What they enjoyed before talk radio and the Internet bloggers came along was a virtual news monopoly, consisting of *The New York Times,* the *Washington Post,* and the three major networks, all of which could be counted on to parrot the liberal line. Now, like spoiled brats being forced to share their toys, they can't stop whining.

Frankly, I'm amazed that liberals can be wrong so often about so many things. One of the few issues they are occasionally right about is protecting the environment. But even when it comes down to that, the radical element that infests their ranks like termites is always trying to stop any and all forms of development, the source of homes and jobs for those of us who don't want to live in trees. Their love for Mother Earth leads them to blow up buildings, bomb car dealerships, and sabotage logging sites, all with an air of moral authority. They don't, in fact, love snail darters, spotted owls, or Alaska's caribou, any more than the rest of us; they merely hate western civilization in much the same way that Islamic fascists do.

A fact worth noting is that during LBJ's administration, a group of tree huggers got an injunction to prevent the feds from working on a certain project in the South, for fear it would harm the environment. The project involved shoring up the levees of New Orleans.

As someone who has spent most of his lifetime working in television, I find it odd that there are two Hollywoods. The famous one is filled with wealthy writers, directors, actors, and production executives, 99% of whom are liberals, all of whom naturally regard themselves as populists, standing shoulder to shoulder with the working stiff. What isn't so widely known is that when it comes to the caste system, whatever its status in modern day India, it's alive and well out here. Go on any movie or TV sound stage and you'll find that among Hollywood's untouchables, those who don't pop up on award shows or in the tabloids — the grips, the costumers, the camera crew, the wranglers, the stunt people, the technicians — the percentage of conservatives is roughly 99%.

I would think the hardest part of being a liberal is always having to remember to spout the party line, just like old-time Stalinists. For instance, they always have to keep in mind that they support our troops even though they believe the men and women in Iraq are spilling innocent blood in an evil war. In the same way, they must always remember to parrot the propaganda that they, every bit as much as conservatives, want a strong military. The basic difference, of course, is that they don't want it to do anything.

Sometimes, people ask me why I invariably identify myself as a conservative and not a Republican. The first, I point out, is a philosophy, while the latter is a political party. A philosophy can afford to be pure as the driven snow. A party, on the other hand, has to deal with the nitty-gritty of fundraising and electing candidates. I accept the realities of politics. Furthermore, I know too much about human nature to ever have my illusions crushed. Unlike my fellow conservatives, I don't believe it when an office seeker of any political persuasion vows he'll cut spending and clear out all the bloated bureaucracies once he or she is elected and goes off to Sacramento, Springfield, Albany, Montgomery, Austin, or, especially, Washington, D.C. It simply goes against every instinct known to man to seek office with the intention of having less money, power, and influence than one's predecessor.

While it's true that I invariably vote for Republicans, I never fool myself into thinking they'll be anything except better than their Democratic opponents. Those people who are hurt by such political facts of life are to be pitied. It's like a child's discovery that Santa Claus and the Easter Bunny aren't who they've been cracked up to be. To such conservatives, all I can say is: Grow up.

Looking back on my own political metamorphosis, I realize how typical it is that, as one matures, takes on responsibilities, and deals with tragedy and loss, one tends to drift from left to right, and how rarely the reverse occurs.

It is hard to dispute the old truism that if, at 20, you're not a liberal, you have no heart; and, if by 40, you're not a conservative, you have no brain. And, it's worth noting that if, by, say, 50, you have neither, you'll probably wind up voting for Ralph Nader.

• 95 •
Marijuana and Me

Apparently, if we're to believe his friend's tape recordings, George W. Bush smoked pot at some time in his life. In some quarters, this president is taking some heat for having actually inhaled. Well, I'm confessing that I, too, smoked a little weed in my younger days. Unlike some people, such as Bill Maher, I'm not bragging about it. It's simply something I did, like riding a bike and practicing my hook shot three hours a day, and now I don't.

Therefore, unlike many of my fellow conservatives, when I discuss marijuana, I've had firsthand experience with it. To begin with, I am certain that, overall, the stuff did me far less harm than the Marlboros I smoked and the vodka I drank in those days. Understand, I am not advocating its use. But I would argue that in a society where I was free to satisfy my cravings for nicotine, which kills thousands of Americans every year, and alcohol, which not only kills and maims thousands of others, but destroys careers, friendships, and families, it is the height of absurdity and hypocrisy to make possession of pot illegal.

Based on my experience with the stuff, along with witnessing its effect on others, I would say it makes people hungry, dozy and stupid. Which sounds like the three dwarfs who didn't get cast opposite Snow White. What it doesn't sound like, and what it isn't, is a societal scourge.

It doesn't make people violent, and it is not so expensive that people have to resort to theft or prostitution in order to pay for it. I have heard people insist that marijuana use leads to cocaine, heroin, meth, ludes, ecstasy, and all those other scary drugs we hear about. That, my friends, is baloney. While it is probably true that every heroin addict at some point smoked some weed, it is ridiculous to suggest that the progression was inevitable. It's like suggesting that some hood driving the getaway car for a gang of bank robbers started out driving to the movies and the mall, and thus doomed himself to a life of vehicular crime.

The problem with outlawing marijuana is that there is simply no upside to its prohibition. It wastes the time of cops, judges, and prosecutors who should be concentrating their efforts on the criminals and sociopaths who actually prey on us. It fills our prisons to overflowing, forcing us to either cough up millions of dollars to build more jails or, in order to make room, offer early releases to the felons who really need to be locked up.

In addition, it keeps the price of the cheap product higher than it otherwise would be for no other reason than that it's illegal.

Also, let us not overlook the fact that it is a major industry, but nobody involved with it — be they growers, distributors or consumers — pays a single dollar in taxes. On the contrary, it drains much-needed tax dollars away from schools, roads, and law enforcement. Talk about dumb!

In addition to everything else, its illegality is preventing people who require it for its various medicinal properties from obtaining it. Talk about cruel!

Lest you think I have written this because I feel the law breathing down my neck, I swear I haven't smoked a joint in more than 40 years. And inasmuch as George Bush apparently broke the law more recently than that, if the narcs come after me, I intend to roll over and give up the president!

You may be wondering why I quit using the stuff. Well, in the beginning, I must admit I enjoyed the reaction I got. It made me feel relaxed and very amusing. It was only later, on those occasions when I hadn't indulged and my friends had, that I discovered how boring and stupid they all sounded. It occurred to me that perhaps, just maybe, marijuana didn't really turn me into Oscar Wilde on one of his wittier days.

Once I decided to quit smoking, I just flushed my few joints down the toilet, and I never felt the slightest urge to ever light up again. Take my word for it, the stuff is about as addictive as cauliflower. However, I did find I had to enter rehab in order to kick the brownie habit.

· 96 ·
Red Sheep

I suspect that every family has its share of skeletons in the closet, black sheep that are only mentioned in passing, in whispers, at Thanksgiving gatherings. In the old days, they might have been horse thieves, rustlers, and card sharks. These days, they're more likely to be defense attorneys, journalists, or judges.

In my own case, most of the black sheep were red. That is to say, they were Communists. Most, if not all, were from my mother's side of the family. Between my uncles and first and second cousins, you could have put together a fairly good-sized cell.

The poorer relatives, many of whom worked in the garment business, cut and sewed for very low wages. Even as a kid, I was able to understand the appeal that Communism held for them. My relatives were Jewish and had been born in czarist Russia, a pigsty of a country notable for its Cossacks and its pogroms. It took the Russian Reds to rid the land of the much-despised Nicholas II. For them, the enemy of their enemies was considered a friend.

After coming to America, they found that it was the Communists who not only talked about the dignity of the working man, but who often got their heads busted by hired goons when they attempted to unionize the sweatshops. I, on the other hand, was born in the U.S. and was well aware that Stalin was every bit as evil as Hitler and every bit as anti-Semitic as Nicholas and the rest of the Romanovs. Still, under the circumstances, I could understand why these folks might not see things my way.

But I had these other relatives, uncles who had made a killing on Chicago's thriving black market during WW II. Once the war ended, they decided that, between Russia and the Windy City, they'd had enough lousy weather to last a lifetime. So in 1946 they moved their families and their ill-gotten gains to Los Angeles, where they proceeded to buy up parking lots, bowling alleys, and apartment houses.

That was bad enough. But having to hear them rhapsodize about Joseph Stalin — Uncle Joe to his friends — and the wonders he had wrought in the Soviet Union used to drive me crazy. Whenever I'd suggest they should consider moving back to the worker's paradise they kept yakking about, they'd just nod sagely and say, "Comes the revolution, America will be another Soviet Union."

Once, when I'd finally had my fill, I said to one of them, "Uncle Meyer, you're not only a very wealthy capitalist, but you made your money as a war profiteer, and now you're making even more as an absentee landlord. For good measure, you're a Jew. Don't you realize that, comes the revolution, the comrades will line you up against the wall and shoot you even before they get around to the Rockefellers?"

If I live to be a hundred, I'll never forget the expression on his face. I have no idea if he was shocked more by my statement or by the fact that his young nephew could not only envision his uncle being executed, but grin about it.

Obviously I don't know how my rich Red relatives carried on when I wasn't around, but at least I never again had to listen to any of *my* uncles sing the praises of *their* uncle.

• 97 •
Long Night's Journey into Day

People often ask me just exactly when I stopped being a liberal and, depending on their own political persuasion, saw the light or sold my soul to the devil. My fellow conservatives assume I had something akin to an epiphany. Liberals simply wonder if I tripped and fell on my head.

When I fail to come up with anything specific, I can invariably read disappointment in their eyes. The truth is that it was a fairly gradual process. I grew up in a typical middle-class Jewish home, the third son of Russian immigrant parents. In other words, Franklin Roosevelt was our patron saint. In our house, the feeling was that he could walk — or at least roll — on water. Then, after FDR's death, when Harry Truman recognized the state of Israel, in 1948, that cinched things. After that, if the Republicans had run God for president, we wouldn't have voted for Him.

So, by the time I got to cast a vote in my first presidential election in 1964, naturally I cast it for Lyndon Johnson. Then, in '68, I voted for Hubert Humphrey. After that, things only got worse. Over the course of the next two decades, I actually voted for McGovern, Carter, Carter, Mondale, and Dukakis. I would say that sounds like the name of a sleazy law firm, but that would be unfair to sleazy law firms. The thing is, even back then, I'd wake up the day after voting for one of these clowns, and I'd hate myself.

Back in the '80s, I was still one of those shmoes who laughed at jokes about Ronald Reagan nodding off during cabinet meetings. Somewhere along the line, though, it began to sink in that the sleepy head had managed to turn around an economy that had a 21% rate of inflation under his predecessor, and, for an encore, managed to end the Cold War. Even a dope like me who had voted for a sanctimonious phony like Jimmy Carter had to admit that was a pretty sensational performance. It turned out that the actor had finally found his perfect role.

Then, in the early 1990s, two things happened that convinced me that I could no longer vote Democratic or identify myself as a liberal, even if it meant that my relatives were going to start spinning in their graves. I could only hope that, were they still alive, they would have felt that being a liberal no longer meant that you opposed the poll tax and segregated lunch counters, but that you were blindly beholden to well-heeled defense attorneys; the morally bankrupt ACLU; and the self-serving likes of Jesse Jackson, Al Sharpton, and Maxine Waters.

From 1987-1991, I served on the Board of Directors of the Writers Guild of America. It was my first hands-on experience in the political arena. I think it's safe to say that of the three officers and sixteen board members, virtually all of us were registered Democrats. A handful of the older members had been blacklisted forty years earlier because they'd been Communists. Nearly everyone in the boardroom, I should hasten to say, was a nice, decent, at least fairly intelligent human being. There were certainly no more than two or three whom I would have gladly fed to the sharks.

Because the agonizing six-month strike of 1988 took place during my first term in office, I had seen my colleagues at their best and at their worst. But it wasn't until one of my last days in office that I realized how far apart I was from the others. The way the by-laws of the WGA were written, the Board could, without putting it to a vote of the membership, elect to bestow sums up to $5,000 to any cause we felt deserving of our largesse.

On this occasion, the defense attorneys for photographer Robert Mapplethorpe had contacted us, requesting that the Guild sign on as amicus curiae in the pornography case that had recently been filed against their client.

Mapplethorpe, in case his name has slipped your mind, had received a grant from the National Endowment of the Arts over the strong objections of North Carolina's Senator Jesse Helms. The senator felt that the U.S. government had no business subsidizing a man who devoted his career to photographing naked children. Naturally, in elite circles, that made Sen. Helms a buffoon, a lunkhead, a southern rube who couldn't tell the difference between a pedophile and an artiste.

When it came time to take a vote that night at the Guild, I was the only person who spoke out against supporting Mapplethorpe legally or financially. In the first place, I never thought the federal government had any business supporting the arts with even a single dollar of tax funds. There were even back then about a quarter of a billion Americans. I figured if an artist couldn't appeal to a sufficient number of that many people to earn an honest living, it wasn't a federal subsidy he required, but vocational guidance.

In the second place, I didn't think the WGA should be wasting the hard-earned money of its members supporting the artistic freedom of some creep who could only have his creative vision satisfied by having an eight- or nine-year-old child stripped down and posed for his camera.

That night, when I was outvoted 18-1, I clearly saw the enormous gulf that separated me from the liberals in the room. It wasn't simply that we disagreed about whether or not to support this guy, either. It was the fact that they didn't even need to consider what I was saying. It was enough that the ACLU was on Mapplethorpe's side and a southern reactionary was opposed. That was really all they needed to know.

The second thing that turned me into a raging Republican? That's easy. After naturally assuming that the Democrats couldn't possibly do any worse after selecting Michael S. Dukakis to be their standard-bearer in 1988, they accomplished that seemingly impossible feat in 1992 by nominating Hillary Rodham Clinton's husband.

• 98 •
A Few Things I Neglected to Say

Recently, I appeared on a San Francisco radio talk show. I had looked forward to discussing a wide range of topics with the host and his callers. That's why I had e-mailed a score of my essays to his producer. But I guess nobody bothered to read any of them. Instead, because the host simply introduced me as the author of *Conservatives Are From Mars, Liberals Are From San Francisco,* virtually every caller for the entire hour wanted to know what I meant by conservative as opposed to Republican and wondered why I insisted that, on most matters, I actually regard myself as a libertarian. Long before the hour was over, thanks to a notoriously low boredom threshold, my eyes had rolled back into my skull and I was gasping for oxygen.

Still, I blame myself for giving incomplete answers to a few of the questions. For instance, I claimed that whereas most people have come to expect the federal government to pay for everything, I feel that the feds should be limited pretty much to waging war and guarding our borders. When I was asked why I felt that way, I don't even recall what I replied. But what I should have said was that I am not an anarchist who is opposed to all forms of government, but the more localized government is, the more accountable it is to the people. For instance, it's fairly easy to remove incompetent mayors and corrupt councilmen, but go try to get rid of Barbara Boxer or Patrick Leahy.

When asked if I really believed that if the federal government wasn't taxing us to death, people would actually take up the slack and give more to charity, I said people definitely would. But I should have gone further. I should have pointed out that, long before there was an income tax, Andrew Carnegie, a personal hero of mine, singlehandedly created the public library system in America. Or I could have said that when I was earning good money in TV, I would pay for my mother-in-law to come out for annual visits from Nebraska. But when the jobs dried up, I no longer was able to fly her to L.A. It only stands to reason that the more money people have, the more generous they can afford to be.

Furthermore, it makes no sense to send our money to Washington, D.C., just so the politicians can dole it out as they see fit.

For one thing, regular charity groups do a better job of it. Most of the money donated to legitimate charities goes to do what the donors intended. But a huge chunk of the money we send to Uncle Sam is skimmed off to finance bloated federal bureaucracies. When a charity behaves that way, the executive director either ends up being fired or in the pokey.

When Americans are flush, they're the most generous people on earth. Look at the flood of dollars they sent to the survivors of 9/11 even though many of those people were already collecting on life insurance policies. Better yet, think of all the money we kicked in after the tsunami hit a part of the world where many, if not most of the people who were victimized, were Islamics who despise America! And of course, in the wake of Katrina, people all over the country are breaking open their piggy banks.

I'm afraid that too many of us have been bamboozled into buying into the notion that the folks in Washington should be encouraged in their attempts at social engineering. It shocks and saddens me that so many Americans see nothing wrong with the federal government encroaching into every area of our lives. For my part, I don't want the feds doling out small business loans, overseeing our schools, ruling on abortions, and I certainly don't want five idiots on the Supreme Court deciding that eminent domain gives the government carte blanche to confiscate our homes and businesses.

Understand, it has nothing to do with whether I agree with what the feds are doing, either. If it's wrong when I disagree with their behavior, it's no less wrong when I happen to be in agreement. It has to do with the sort of country this is supposed to be. If I wanted socialism, I would vote for socialists or move to Sweden.

One of my callers, by the way, said she was all for a socialistic government. I asked her why she thought that would be a good thing. She replied that people who had more would then have to share with people who had less. I said that I, along with the majority of people I knew, was in favor of sharing, but once it stopped being done on a voluntary basis, it was no longer sharing, it was Communism.

Frankly, I'm afraid that's where we're headed. I suppose it began back in the '30s when Roosevelt and Congress got together and created that alphabet soup of federal agencies. Ever since, Americans have grown more and more accustomed to Washington's usurping individual responsibility. As a result, we have become a nation of brats. We whine when the price of gas goes up and accept it as our birthright when it goes down. It's as if we think we have a sacred right to pay the same price for fuel as our ancestors. In the meantime, without a squawk, we pay an arm and a leg for bottled water, $3.50 for a box of movie theatre popcorn, and of course we keep right on buying cars the size of Sherman tanks.

Like teenagers, we expect Uncle Sam to pay for all the essentials, such as health care and housing, while we blithely blow our allowances on such pricey toys as oversized TVs and cable service, cell phones, DVD players, Nintendo games, and $125 sneakers for the kids.

We even have the attention span of children. We get into a war and immediately demand to know when it will be over — like little kids in the back seat incessantly asking if we're there yet. Can you imagine anybody inquiring of FDR, in 1943, if he had a timetable for withdrawing from North Africa or Italy or Corregidor?

When a caller wanted me to explain how, without federal assistance, New Orleans could be expected to cope in the aftermath of Katrina, I said that catastrophic insurance might have helped. Or perhaps if the state or city had built stronger levees, the entire tragedy could have been avoided. In any case, other cities have managed to rebuild without the federal government staking out ever more turf. Chicago managed to come back from a holocaust, and San Francisco recovered nicely from its earthquake. I am for relying on private enterprise and the generosity of individual Americans. After all, the only money the feds have is what it takes from us. It's not as if George Bush is writing a personal check on his Crawford account.

Honestly, I don't know how our parents and grandparents, members of what has been labeled the Greatest Generation for the gallant way they dealt with the Depression and World War II, can stomach us. They have us over for Thanksgiving, and we're bigger turkeys than the bird in the oven.

That's what I should have said.

• 99 •
The Flag and Me

In the days and weeks following 9/11, friends and neighbors saw the American flag flying by my front door and assumed it was in remembrance of the people murdered by Islamic terrorists. I didn't bother correcting them because, by then, that was certainly part of my intention. The thing is, the flag had been out there for several months, but they just hadn't noticed. Or maybe they just thought it was corny and didn't want to comment. But, now, I think, is a good time to set the record straight.

I went out and bought the flag because of my grandparents. I should explain I had never known my dad's parents, both of whom died before I was born. I knew my mother's parents, but could never speak to them. Although they had come to America in 1921, they never learned English. They could speak Russian and Hebrew, but they preferred Yiddish. I couldn't converse in any of those languages. And, so, to me, my grandmother was this little old woman who would give me a wet kiss on the cheek and slip a quarter into my hand. My grandfather was a very quiet, bearded man who always wore a black frock coat; he looked like a short Abe Lincoln. He went to shul twice a day. When he was home, he was either reading the Torah, shelling lima beans or sipping tea through a sugar cube held between his front teeth. In short, if my life were a movie, they'd have been dress extras.

So why did I buy a flag because of those four people — two of whom I had never met and two of whom I had never spoken to? It's simple. Because of sheer, unadulterated gratitude.

You see, one day, on my way home, I began to think how lucky I was to have been born in this country. Through no effort of my own, having made no sacrifice, taken no risk, I was the beneficiary of freedom, liberty, education, comfort, security, and yes, even luxury. It was not the first time I had acknowledged this good fortune. The difference this time is that, for some reason, it suddenly occurred to me that my good luck hadn't just happened. It had been the direct result of these four people pulling up stakes and moving thousands of miles, across an entire continent and the Atlantic Ocean, to a new country, pursuing a dream that their children and their children's children, of whom I am one, might, just might have better lives.

There were no guarantees. That was my epiphany. They had been denied the assurances of hindsight. They had done all this on a roll of the dice, only knowing for certain that there would be no going back.

My father's parents were illiterate peasants. My mother's parents not only never spoke a word of English, but her father — although he owned a small grocery store in Chicago — never, in 30 years, spoke on a telephone because he didn't want to embarrass himself. But their grandson, bless their hearts, has enjoyed a career as a successful writer. I doubt if any of them imagined anything so specific or anything quite that wonderful when they snuck across the Romanian border in the dead of night, but they had certainly heard a rumor that in America anything was possible.

The fact is, had those four people, all of whom were poor and barely, if at all, educated — their little children in tow — not somehow found the courage to make the journey, I would have been born a Jew in the Soviet Union. Between Stalin and Hitler, the odds are likely I would have wound up a slave in Siberia or a bar of German soap.

So it happened that day when I was out driving and thought about the enormous debt I owed those four immigrants, a debt I could never possibly repay, I decided to pull in at the local hardware store and buy a flag. I thought it was something they'd have wanted me to do on their behalf. It wasn't nearly enough, I know, but it was something.

• 100 •

Bargaining with the Devil

Perhaps it's this way with most writers, but in my life books have often played a larger role than have people. Filled with wisdom, joy, tears, and laughter, they are everything parents, friends, and siblings should be but rarely are. And very early on, one book in particular taught me a lesson I have never forgotten.

It all began on a Saturday afternoon in 1951. One of my older brothers took me to see a re-issue of *The Grapes of Wrath*. It wasn't my usual movie fare, but the saga of the Joads losing their home to the Oklahoma dust storms struck a major chord. Maybe in my eleven-year-old brain, I made a connection to our own move west from Chicago to Los Angeles a few years earlier. Or maybe it was just the natural empathy anybody would have for decent people whose lives were tragically uprooted through no fault of their own. If it could happen to the Joads, it could happen to anyone.

In any case, when we got home, I noticed a thick volume with the same title on the bookshelf. I decided to read it. The novel was probably three or four times longer than anything I had ever tried. But I wanted to know more about those people. Maybe I was hoping the book, unlike the movie, had a happy ending.

Two weeks later I turned in a report to my teacher, Mr. Vanderhaven. I assumed he'd be impressed that someone who had never exhibited much interest in reading anything that didn't have Oz or Dolittle in its title had actually read and appreciated a 600-page novel about migrant farm workers. He was impressed beyond my wildest dreams. He gave me an A+. Next to the grade, however, was a question mark.

When I asked him about it, Mr. Vanderhaven explained he could not enter the grade in his roll book until I made one small change. It seems I had described one of the characters, Rosasharn, as "pregnant." The word, he said, was unacceptable in the fifth grade. Acceptable terms for her condition, he told me, were "full of life" or "in a family way." I thought he was kidding. He wasn't.

What made his reaction particularly mystifying was that he was the first male teacher I had ever had. I'd have been less surprised if prissy Miss Crane or Mrs. Gordon, my third- and fourth-grade teachers, had taken me to task. But Mr. Vanderhaven?! Besides, the book report wasn't for public consumption. The only people whose sensibilities could possibly be offended by that wicked eight-letter word were Vanderhaven and myself. And it was too late to save either of us.

I must have voiced some mild defense of my position because, for the first time in my school life, I was sent home with a note to my mother. When I presented my case to her, she told me to shape up and give Mr. Vanderhaven what he wanted.

The next day the dirty deed was done. Rosasharn was no longer pregnant; she was something else, but I can't recall what. All I can recall after all these years is that I got my A+, but I thought it scarlet and shameful.

In a roundabout way, *The Grapes of Wrath* taught me what great books always do. It showed me who I was — an eleven year old wimp, a groveler for grades. But, more important, it made me realize who and what I wanted to be. A's, I learned, are cheap, but principles are dear. It was the last time as a writer or as a person I ever consciously betrayed my own convictions.

The lesson I came away with, thanks to the unlikely combination of Steinbeck and Vanderhaven, is that when you sell out, you inevitably get less than you bargained for — whether you're Faust or a fifth-grader.

• 101 •
Elegy, 1969

Two days ago, I returned from a weekend in San Francisco to learn that my father had died. Sam Prelutsky had been born in Russia, in 1901 or 1902. He never knew for certain. It didn't seem to bother him.

As a young man in America, he settled in a part of Illinois where the most popular organization around was the Ku Klux Klan. After the Cossacks, though, I guess a bunch of farmers wearing sheets wasn't such a big deal. Years later, he used to laugh about his former neighbors inviting him — *him* with his nose and his name and his accent — on Klan outings. Maybe they decided to overlook the obvious evidence of his ethnicity in the belief that Jewish people didn't raise chickens and candle eggs.

Later, after he was married, he moved to Chicago. For a while, he worked for a cigar company, rolling the stogies he couldn't stand to smoke. But for most of the time he was a fruit and vegetable wholesaler. He'd drive his truck to the big central market at 3 a.m., pick up his load, and spend the next twelve hours delivering produce. In the dead of winter, he'd be out on that truck shlepping sacks of potatoes. In the middle of summer, he'd be muscling crates of watermelons — just begging for the hernia he eventually got.

We moved to L.A. in 1946. At that point he came to the conclusion that the people he'd been delivering to over the years had been living the life of Riley, home in bed snoozing while he was up shlepping. He decided to tackle the retail end. A few months at a bad location ate up most of his savings and sent him back to the truck.

But L.A., massive sprawl that it was even then, was murder compared to the more compact Chicago.

His next venture was a cigar stand in the Harris-Newmark Building at Ninth and Los Angeles. Not counting the drive downtown, it was still a twelve-hour day, spent mostly on his feet. But at least the lifting and hauling was limited to soft-drink cases and trash barrels. On the other hand, you had to learn to live with the *goniffs* who swiped candy bars during the noon rush and the merchant princes of the garment industry who'd run up good-sized cigar bills and let you stew until they were ready to pay up. And my father would stew because he couldn't afford to offend the potbellied, cigar-chewing, fanny-pinching sweatshop aristocrats.

He was not an educated man. He couldn't correctly spell the names of those sodas and candy bars he sold six days a week. I don't know if he read two dozen books in his life. He loved America, Israel, pinochle, FDR, and the Democratic party. He liked Willkie, Kuchel and Warren; but he could never bring himself to vote for a Republican.

It was because of my father that when I switched my allegiance to the conservative wing of the GOP, it was with some misgiving. I couldn't help wondering what he would have thought. Would he have seen it as a betrayal of everything he held dear? Would he have regarded it as the act of a turncoat, as some of my erstwhile friends did? After thinking long and hard about it, I decided that he might have made the switch even earlier than I did. It was the party, after all, that had turned its back on people like my dad, immigrants who had worked hard all their lives to earn a place in America's middle class only to see the liberals in Washington do everything in their power to push them down into what I call the dependent class.

My dad wanted me to get good grades, a college degree and have a profession — something safe and preferably lucrative, like medicine or the law. He couldn't understand someone's wanting to write for a living. Still, when I sold a poem for fifty cents at the age of thirteen, he cashed the check for me — and much, much later I found out that forever after he carried that check folded up in his wallet.

Yesterday, we went to the mortuary. We went through the ritual of selecting a casket. "They start at $300," the salesman informed us, pointing at something that looked like an old Thom McAn shoe box, "and go up." We passed on the coffin that cost as much as a new Cadillac, and settled on an oak box that you could swap for a '65 Chevy.

Then we had to sit there while some woman gathered data for the cosmetician. We tried to explain that it was to be a closed-casket ceremony, but she had not been programmed to receive such information. "Did he wear clear nail polish?" (No, he never wore nail polish. But had he worn nail polish, it would have been clear as opposed to purple or fire-engine red!)

It was finally spelled out for her that they could save their rouge and polish and stupid questions. She turned pale at our impertinence. Her shock was reassuring; she was not a robot, after all.

We buried my father this afternoon. I didn't think I would, but I shed tears. I cried because he had worked too hard for too long for too little. For many years, I had resented him because he had never told me he loved me; now I wept because I'd never told him.

The rabbi's speech was short and simple. What is there, after all, to say at the funeral of such a man? Had the responsibility been mine, I would have said: Sam Prelutsky, who was born in a small village 7,000 miles from here, 67 or 68 years ago, was a remarkable person. He was not a great man or a famous man, but he was the best man Sam Prelutsky could be. Now, let there be no more tears today, for we are laying to rest a man who's earned one.